Migration, Accommodation and Language Change

Palgrave Macmillan Studies in Language Variation

The study of language variation in social context, and the study of specific language communities in detail, are central to the linguistic enterprise. In this series we look for impressive first-hand fieldwork from speech communities of various kinds, analysed within a range of frameworks, quantitative and qualitative. All work reported in the series will raise important arguments about methodologies for researching language in social context, with analysis that challenges or extends current theory building.

Titles include:

Bridget L. Anderson
MIGRATION, ACCOMMODATION AND LANGUAGE CHANGE
Language at the Intersection of Regional and Ethnic Identity

Jonathan Marshall
LANGUAGE CHANGE AND SOCIOLINGUISTICS
Rethinking Social Networks

Daniel Schreier
ISOLATION AND LANGUAGE CHANGE
Contemporary and Sociohistorical Evidence from Tristan da Cunha English

Palgrave Macmillan Studies in Language Variation
Series Standing Order ISBN 1–4039–1198–3
(*outside North America only*)

You can receive future titles in this series as they are published by placing a standing order. Please contact your bookseller or, in case of difficulty, write to us at the address below with your name and address, the title of the series and the ISBN quoted above.

Customer Services Department, Macmillan Distribution Ltd, Houndmills, Basingstoke, Hampshire RG21 6XS, England

Migration, Accommodation and Language Change

Language at the Intersection of Regional and Ethnic Identity

Bridget L. Anderson
Old Dominion University

First published 2008 by
PALGRAVE MACMILLAN
Houndmills, Basingstoke, Hampshire RG21 6XS and
175 Fifth Avenue, New York, N.Y. 10010
Companies and representatives throughout the world

PALGRAVE MACMILLAN is the global academic imprint of the Palgrave Macmillan division of St. Martin's Press, LLC and of Palgrave Macmillan Ltd. Macmillan® is a registered trademark in the United States, United Kingdom and other countries. Palgrave is a registered trademark in the European Union and other countries.

ISBN-13: 978–0–230–00886–1 hardback
ISBN-10: 0–230–00886–0 hardback

This book is printed on paper suitable for recycling and made from fully managed and sustained forest sources. Logging, pulping and manufacturing processes are expected to conform to the environmental regulations of the country of origin.

A catalogue record for this book is available from the British Library.

Library of Congress Cataloging-in-Publication Data
Anderson, Bridget L., 1972–
    Migration, accommodation and language change:language at the intersection of regional and ethnic identity/Bridget L. Anderson.
        p.   cm. — (Palgrave studies in language variation series)
    Includes index.
    ISBN-10: 0–230–00886–0 (alk. paper)
    ISBN-13: 978–0–230–00886–1
    1. English language—Variation—United States.   2. English language—Dialects—United States.   3. English language—Social aspects—United States.   I. Title.
PE2841.A215 2008
427'.973—dc22
                                                                2007048692

10   9   8   7   6   5   4   3   2   1
17   16   15   14   13   12   11   10   09   08

Printed and bound in Great Britain by
CPI Antony Rowe, Chippenham and Eastbourne

This book, my first, is dedicated to my teachers: Walt Wolfram, Lesley Milroy, Patrice Speeder Beddor, Erik Thomas, Jose Benki, and Judith Irvine. Fieldwork, ethnography, vowels, methods, coarticulation, dialect contact, language ideology... I learned so much from all of you!

Contents

List of Figures

List of Tables

Acknowledgments

My first thanks goes to the participants in this study, who opened up their homes to me and made this research possible. My second thanks goes to my teachers, to whom I have dedicated this book. In particular, Walt Wolfram, Lesley Milroy, Pam Beddor, and Erik Thomas have all uniquely contributed to my development as a scholar and have guided me through graduate school and beyond. I am blessed with the best mentors the universe has to offer! I also want to mention Michael Montgomery. My work has benefited very much from his advice through the years, as well as his excellent example. Michael, I am your biggest fan!

My mother assisted a great deal with the fieldwork with the Appalachian migrants. My parents have been very supportive of my crazy academic lifestyle, including the very long time I spent writing this book. My dear friend Tom Welker helped me reformat the charts and graphs, with all their phonetic fonts, and has my eternal gratitude. The presence of Jen Nguyen, my long-time collaborator, is felt throughout this book. In particular, being able to extensively cite our 2006 paper, which employed the same methods used in this book, made the analysis much deeper and richer. Jen, if I could give you a "best collaborator" award, I would!

I also want to mention some of my colleagues at Old Dominion University. Joanne Scheibman, in particular, spent many hours discussing ethnography and language ideology with me. Joanne is one of those rare people who is so insightful, and so careful in terms of her analysis and thinking, that I felt the need to write down almost everything she told me. I have pages of notes from conversations with her about this book. I also want to mention Janet Bing, who is one of the lights in my professional life. I also want to mention my Chair, David Metzger, and my Dean, Chandra de Silva. Their support during my whole time at Old Dominion, but especially while I was writing this book, is gratefully acknowledged! Dean de Silva provided funding for a fieldwork coordinator for my *Tidewater Voices* project while this book was in the final stages, so that I could focus on finishing it. I am fortunate to have found such a supportive environment, where I can be free in my scholarship and in my thinking.

I thank the external reviewer for this book for insightful comments and helpful advice. I also thank John Baugh for his feedback on the language ideological analysis at the Perspectives on Language Variation Symposium at St Louis University in Fall 2005. His advice resulted in a richer ethnographic analysis. I thank Mark Arehart for his assistance with the statistical analysis.

Finally, I thank my editor, Jill Lake, who I first met when I presented the very first bit of this work (from the pilot study!) in Bristol at the University of the West of England at the Sociolinguistics Symposium 2000. Jill, I want you to know how much your support and encouragement all these years has meant to me, and I thank you for your interest in this work. Jill, your personal qualities, in addition to your professional qualities, make you a rare and special person. I want you to know that I will never forget your many kindnesses! I also thank Melanie Blair for her hard work and support during this process. How blessed I am that she and Jill were the editorial team for my first book!

1
Introduction

In the early decades of the twentieth century, large numbers of African American and White Southerners migrated from the rural South to the urban Midwest to work in factories (Berry 2000). Although these two migrant groups are separated by ethnicity, they share a regional affiliation with the South as well as Southern cultural characteristics (Anderson 2003). This situation provides an unique opportunity to examine ways in which the interaction of ethnicity and regional affiliation gives rise to systematic patterns of language variation and change and phonetic restructuring as a result of language contact. Patterns of use have been shown by sociolinguistic researchers to provide a window into group solidarity and ethnic identity, as well as to index social and linguistic relations within and among groups. A dramatic example of such indexicality is provided in the Midwestern cities by the distinctiveness of African American English (AAE) from Midwestern White varieties.

This investigation of the dialect contact situation between African American and Appalachian White Southern migrant groups and their descendants in the Detroit metropolitan area provides an explanation of the continuing distinctiveness of Southern migrant vowel patterns from those of Midwestern Whites in the city. Linguistic effects of large-scale migration for these two Southern groups across three generations of speakers are described and compared to the surrounding dialect norms of Midwestern Whites, through acoustic analysis of portions of the vowel systems.

The aims of this study are as follows. First, the study provides a description of portions of the vowel systems of six Detroit

African American and six Appalachian Southern migrant participants. Second, it provides a detailed analysis of the changes taking place in the vowel systems and attempts to contextualize the phonetic data both historically, with reference to the data collected by Wolfram in 1969, and within an account of local language ideology. Third, the results are evaluated with reference to current models of change in vowel systems, especially the principles of internal change proposed by Labov (1994). The effects of leveling in this dialect contact situation are also addressed. Finally, the relationship between internal constraints on and external motivations for language change is examined in a framework that is sensitive to contextual, or coarticulatory, effects from the following consonant on patterns of use.

The methodology is a combination of techniques used in variationist sociolinguistics and acoustic phonetics. The fieldwork with the African American participants and one of the Appalachian Southern migrant participants took place in inner city Detroit and in the adjacent inner suburbs of Warren, Taylor, Royal Oak, and Dearborn Heights with the rest of the Appalachian White participants. Data was extracted from 60 minutes of sociolinguistic interviews for each participant for the acoustic analysis, the methods of which are described in Chapter 5.

I analyze the acoustic results with particular reference to local language ideologies and ideological stances which emerged during the data collection phase of the study. I argue in Chapter 8 that vowel changes are internally constrained but subject to ideological intervention. Specifically, I argue that the fronting of /u/ and /ʊ/ is part of a widespread phonetic change taking place in many varieties of English around the world and no longer provide a "crucial site" (Phillips 2000: 233) used to express a local orientation for the Southern migrant participants in this study. In contrast, glide-weakened /ai/ functions as a socially salient ethnolinguistic boundary marker that is rich in local meaning. The results from the acoustic study indicate that, for middle-aged and younger African American participants, glide-weakening has expanded its territory to include the progressive pre-voiceless context. I associate both the fronting of the high and lower-high back vowels and pre-voiceless /ai/ glide-weakening, changes which have only recently been reported for African American speakers, with changes in the sociolinguistic landscapes of speakers following migration from the rural South to the urban Midwest. The social group which became most relevant—the group from which African American and Appalachian participants saw themselves as most distinctive—were White Midwesterners. Furthermore, both groups display orientations to the South in culturally important ways. A linguistic alignment to a Southern norm which does not clearly distinguish between AAE and White Southern varieties therefore can be described in relation to the complex attitudes and ideologies emerging after migration.

This book consists of nine chapters. Chapter 2 surveys the work on language variation and change which underpins the study. Chapter 3 describes the research site, the history of migration of Southern migrants to Southeastern Michigan, and gives overviews of Appalachian English and AAE in both Southern and Midwestern (urban) contexts. Chapter 4 describes the pilot study. Chapter 5 describes field techniques, sociolinguistic methods, and acoustic methods. Chapter 6 gives the acoustic results for the high and lower-high vowels, and Chapter 7 gives the results for the low vowels. Chapter 8 situates the acoustic results within local and supralocal contexts, and situates the patterns of use revealed by the acoustic analysis with reference to local language ideologies which emerged during the fieldwork phase of the study. Chapter 9 discusses the limitations and contributions of the study and also gives an assessment of the broader implications of the study.

2
Empirical and Theoretical Background

In this chapter I discuss the empirical and theoretical issues that inform this study. Several questions and intellectual problems guided this research. First, I was skeptical of the claim that African Americans do not participate in any of the large-scale vowel rotations in American English (e.g. Labov 1994, 2001; Bailey and Thomas 1998; Thomas 2001). Wolfram (2007) characterizes the assumption that "... regionality in African American English is invariably trumped by the trans-regional, common core of shared vernacular traits" as a myth and also labels this assumption as the "exotic variety syndrome." It is important to investigate the extent to which speakers of AAE do or do not participate in contemporary vowel changes in American English. To this end, I investigated the patterning of /u/ and /ʊ/ for the Southern migrant participants in this study. Fronting of these vowels is widespread in American English (see Section 2.1.5). I also examine a more local change for the African American participants in this study, the glide-weakening of /ai/ in the pre-voiceless context, a change that—until recently—was associated with progressive Southern White, but not African American, varieties. Second, I wanted to employ a framework which used local categories relevant to speakers rather than categories imposed by the researcher. Third, I investigate the relationship between internal constraints on and external motivations for language change in a framework that is sensitive to the influences of coarticulation. Socioacoustic work that considers context effects such as coarticulation is also rare.

The structure of the chapter is as follows. Section 2.1 describes vowel changes in progress in American English, including work on the Northern Cities Chain Shift (NCS), the Southern Shift, African American vowel systems, /ai/ glide-weakening, and fronting of the high and lower-high back vowels. Section 2.2 discusses socially oriented frameworks which can help illuminate patterns of vowel changes.

2.1 American English vowel shifts in progress

Following Labov (1991), the major American English dialects have been frequently described in terms of three major vowel rotations: the NCS, the Southern Shift, and a vowel system which merges /ɑ/ and /ɔ/.

2.1.1 The Northern Cities Chain Shift

The NCS is reported as operating in the region stretching from Western New England to the northern tier of Pennsylvania, Northern Ohio, Indiana, Illinois, Michigan, and Wisconsin (Wolfram and Schilling-Estes 1998: 237). Several linguistic researchers (e.g. Labov 1994; Wolfram and Schilling-Estes 1998; Gordon 2001) describe the shift as being most evident in the larger metropolitan areas. Wolfram and Schilling-Estes (1998) and Labov (1991) also observe that younger speakers in the metropolitan areas show the most advanced stages of these changes.

Labov (1994) describes the raising of /æ/ as the oldest change in the NCS and the fronting of /ɑ/ and the lowering and fronting of /ɔ/ as "midrange" changes, and suggests that the three changes therefore constitute a drag chain (Labov 1994: 195). Other changes include the lowering of /ɪ/ and /ɛ/ (not shown in Figure 2.1), which Labov

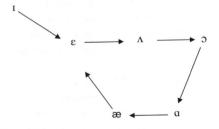

Figure 2.1 The Northern Cities Shift (after Labov 1994: 191)

(1994: 195) describes as "most likely" forming another drag chain. Finally, the backing of /ɛ/ and /ʌ/ forms another link, which Labov describes as a push chain. Labov illustrates the pattern of the NCS as follows. The arrows indicate directions of vowel movement within articulatory space.

The defining characteristic of a chain shift is that each "slot" in the vowel space left empty by a vowel which has moved to another spot will be filled by another vowel participating in the chain rotation. Labov (1994) reports that the NCS is the most complex chain shift yet recorded within one subsystem, involving six members of the English vowel system in one continuous and connected pattern. Labov (1994) cites early evidence for the NCS throughout the Northern dialect area as mapped by Kurath and McDavid in 1961 and Marckwardt in 1957, and notes that the shift was first explicitly proposed in an unpublished paper by Fasold in 1969.

Section 2.1.2 describes the Southern Shift, which is reported to be in progress in White varieties in the American South. One question this study will attempt to answer is why the African American and Appalachian White Southern migrants in this study are not participating in the vowel patterns associated with the NCS but appear to be participating in sound changes currently in progress in the American South such as glide-weakening of pre-voiceless /ai/ and also in changes which are widespread in American English such as the fronting of the high and lower-high back vowels. Particularly, why are the Southern migrant speakers who are Detroit-born apparently participating in these sound changes?

2.1.2 The Southern Shift

The Southern Shift, pictured in Figure 2.2, constitutes a series of sound changes that are said to have moved to virtual completion in Southern White varieties (Bailey and Thomas 1998: 304). Thomas (2001: 1) describes the Southern Shift as involving the fronting of /u/, /ʊ/, and /o/; lowering of the nucleus of /e/ and sometimes the nuclei of /i/ and /u/; fronting and raising of /ɪ/ and /ɛ/, and either the monophthongization or glide-reduction of /ai/ to [aː] or [aᵃ]. Some Southern varieties such as those spoken on the outer banks of North Carolina show backing and raising for the /ai/ nucleus, where it is realized as [ʌɪ] (Schilling-Estes 1996). Thomas (2001: 106) notes that the fronting of /u/ is an old Southern feature, citing Kurath

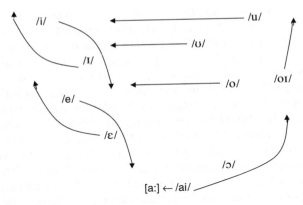

Figure 2.2 Vowel configuration of the Southern Shift (adapted from Labov, 1991)

and McDavid (1961). Thomas also describes the fronting of the /o/ nucleus as a recent change. Labov suggests that the fronting of /o/ has no connection with chain shifting but operates in coordination with the fronting of /u/, lagging "considerably behind it" (1994: 208).

Stockwell and Minkova (1999: 7) describe the vowel changes involved in the Southern Shift differently and argue that these vowel changes should not be presented as part of a chain shift. Fridland (1999) also suggests that the Southern Shift is a set of changes affecting subsystems rather than a unitary chain shift.

2.1.3 African American vowel systems

Labov (1991) describes the AAE system as incompatible with any of the three major vowel rotations in American English (the two vowel shifts described above plus a pattern which merges /ɑ/ and /ɔ/), thus constituting a "fourth dialect." Labov (1998: 147) suggests that AAE is best viewed as a koiné which developed when speakers migrated to the North and Midland urban areas. According to this scenario, some features of Southern phonology were lost and the system leveled to a general Northern African American phonology in which some features of Southern phonology are retained as optional markers of style. Labov does not, however, analyze Northern AAE as a contact variety.

Many researchers agree that AAE norms are diverging from those of White dialects. Thomas (2001: 166) suggests, "for the most part, . . . assimilation to Southern White vernaculars seems to be old-fashioned in African American speech, and younger African Americans are moving toward nationwide norms for African Americans." Wolfram and Schilling-Estes also point out that there is little evidence that the NCS is spreading to AAE speakers in metropolitan areas affected by this shift (1998: 180). Graff *et al.* (1986), Labov and Harris (1986), and Labov (1991, 2001) describe African American vowels as not affected by sound changes occurring in White varieties. Gordon (2000) found the same pattern in Gary, Indiana. Thomas (2001) also reports a pattern in which African Americans do not participate in contemporary White vowel changes. Bailey and Thomas (1998: 95) also suggest that African American speakers are not participating in any of the changes associated with the Southern Shift (except for the glide-weakening of /ai/ in restricted contexts) or the NCS. Several researchers, then, have suggested that African American speakers are not participating in large-scale contemporary vowel changes in American English.

There is some evidence, however, that African Americans do in fact participate in sound changes which are typically associated with White varieties. Thomas (1993) found that African Americans in Columbus, Ohio, showed accommodation to some local vowel changes, including the fronting of /o/. Deser (1990) found that Detroit African Americans were participating in some local White vowel patterns. Jones and Preston (in press) and Jones (MS) reported raising of /æ/ but not fronting of /ɑ/ (both changes associated with the NCS, see Section 2.1.1) among African American women in Lansing, Michigan. Wolfram *et al.* (2000) and Wolfram and Thomas (2002) found that older African Americans in the rural coastal community of Hyde County, North Carolina, showed assimilation to the local White vowel systems.

As noted above, Wolfram (2007) strongly cautions against treating AAE as a unitary, homogenous variety that shows no regional and other kinds of intra-variety variation. The analysis presented in Chapters 6 and 7 will demonstrate that the African American participants in this study show evidence of at least three patterns of use typically associated with White speakers—the fronting of the high and lower-high back vowels /u/ and /ʊ/ and the glide-weakening of pre-voiceless /ai/—and it underscores the importance of recognizing that non-Whites can and do participate in both supralocal, widespread vowel changes as well as more regionally based changes.

2.1.4 /ai/

/ai/ realizations are salient markers of regional and ethnic identity in American English (Anderson 1998, 1999, 2002; Wolfram and Schilling-Estes 1998; Plichta and Preston 2003); pre-voiced monophthongal [a:] and glide-weakened variants such as [aᵃᵉ] are characteristic of both Southern American English and AAE. Bailey and Thomas (1998: 104) point out that originally Southern White varieties were diphthongal for variants of /ai/ and suggest that the innovation and spread of monophthongal and glide-weakened variants may have been the result of influence from early AAE. Tillery and Bailey (2003: 168), citing Bailey and Thomas (1998) and Thomas (2001), describe glide-weakened /ai/ as a change which developed after 1875 in Southern White varieties.

The work of Bailey *et al.* (1996), Bailey and Thomas (1998), Bernstein and Gregory (1993, 1994), and others indicates that /ai/ is monophthongized or glide-weakened throughout the South by both contemporary White and African American speakers in all contexts except before voiceless obstruents. Bailey and Thomas (1998: 104) report that this feature has been shared by African American and Southern White dialects for at least the past 100 years, but that glide-weakening of /ai/ before voiceless obstruents is a relatively recent change specific to some Southern White systems, such as Appalachian and Texas varieties of English. Wolfram and Schilling-Estes (1998: 180) also describe the glide-weakening of /ai/ in pre-voiceless contexts as characteristic of some Southern White, but not AAE, dialects. Although recent work by Mallinson *et al.* (2001) and Childs (2005) on AAE in the Smoky Mountains of Western North Carolina and Fridland (2004) in Memphis suggests that actual language behavior with respect to /ai/ glide-weakening may be more complex than these generalizations suggest, the vowel appears to be treated as a stereotypical marker of ethnic identity (Wolfram and Schilling-Estes 1998; Thomas 2001; Wolfram and Thomas 2002). Based on extensive community language studies in rural North Carolina conducted by the North Carolina Language and Life team at North Carolina State

University, Wolfram and Schilling-Estes (1998: 75) comment on the social salience of Southern variants of /ai/:

> Southerners are more readily identified as Southerners by their /ai/ vowels than by any other single dialect feature, and Southerners themselves have come to take pride in their distinctive pronunciations as a badge of their unique regional identity and cultural heritage.

Wolfram (personal communication) reports that African Americans in the South use a high rate of glide-weakened /ai/ in pre-voiceless contexts in imitations of White speech, and recent work by his own research group confirms the social salience of Southern variants of /ai/ in the South (Wolfram and Thomas 2002). Southern variants of /ai/, however, are also socially salient outside the South. Plichta and Preston's (2003) perceptual study of /ai/ demonstrates that Midwestern Whites rate glide-weakened tokens as characteristic of Southern speech. These researchers describe Southern variants of /ai/ as "one of the principal caricatures of US regional speech." Preston (1996) shows that Southern speech is described as "incorrect" by listeners from around the country. Stimuli in that perceptual and attitudinal study included words containing the socially salient glide-weakened variant of /ai/ in addition to other Southern features.

I will argue in Chapter 8 that /ai/ provides a crucial site for the expression of local language ideologies. Phillips (2000: 233) describes "crucial site" as a term used to " . . . convey the sense that more important or powerful ideological work is being done in some forms of cultural activities than in others." The notion reflects the tendency for " . . . some kinds of linguistic practices . . . (as) more likely to be talked about in metapragmatic commentary than others" (233). As noted above, the use of the Southern glide-weakened variant of /ai/ is socially salient, both in the South and elsewhere. This feature of my own Appalachian speech was frequently commented on during the four years I lived in Michigan.

Midwestern Whites show a different trajectory of change for /ai/ than Southerners, which is also socially salient. Eckert (1996) reports backing and raising of the nucleus of pre-voiceless /ai/ ("Canadian Raising") for suburban Detroit White adolescents. She describes "extreme" raising for /ai/ as being highly socially salient. Eckert's work on /ai/ makes it clear that Detroit Whites in her study show very different realizations of /ai/ than the Southern migrant participants in this study. We shall also see in Chapter 7 that the Detroit White female participant in my sample shows a high degree of diphthongization for /ai/, which is in contrast to the glide-weakening evident in the patterns of use by the Detroit Southern migrant participants. Several researchers have described /ai/ as showing massive variation among different groups of speakers in the Detroit area (Deser 1990; Eckert 1996; Edwards 1997), which suggests that it serves as an important linguistic boundary marker in Detroit.

When compared to other vowels /ai/ is unusual in terms of the complexity of its phonetic and phonological dimensions. According to Labov, /ai/ is unusual in that it may occupy either peripheral or non-peripheral space, resulting in great synchronic variability and complex diachronic movement. Labov suggests that peripheral vowels show different movement patterns than non-peripheral vowels (1991, 1994), but there is some disagreement as to what exactly constitutes peripherality. According to Labov, "in general long vowels are located at the periphery of the vowel space . . . " (1994: 173). Short, or lax vowels, according to this scenario, are more centralized. The concept of peripherality is important to Labov's (1994) claims about chain shifting. Stockwell and Minkova (1997: 2) argue that what Labov characterizes as peripheral diphthongs are actually non-peripheral and vice-versa. Labov (1994) also suggests that monophthongization of /ai/ sets off a vowel rotation for the front vowels, in which /i/ and /ɪ/ are reversed, as well as /e/, and /ɛ/, as part of the Southern Shift.

This section described /ai/ glide-weakening as a local change specific to Southern and African American varieties of English. The next section turns to a more global change in English vowel systems, fronting of the high and lower-high back vowels.

2.1.5 The high and lower-high back vowels /u/ and /ʊ/

In his discussion of vowel variants in New World Englishes, Thomas (2001: 32) describes /ʊ/ as backed in many dialects but fronted in Southern White speech. Thomas characterizes /u/, like /ʊ/, not only as showing variation mainly for the front/back dimension but also as showing variation for the direction of the offglide (33). He does not discuss the details of variation for the offglide. He describes widespread fronting of /u/ among Whites, citing his own studies of central Ohio (Thomas 1993), Habick's study of central Illinois (1980, 1993), Labov's (1994) study of Philadelphia, Luthin's study of California (1987), Ash's study of the Inland Upper North (1996), and Clarke *et al.*'s study of New England and Canada (1995). African Americans, however, are generally said not to participate in widespread vowel changes in American English, including the fronting of /u/ and /ʊ/ (Labov 1994, 2001; Wolfram and Schilling-Estes 1998; Thomas 2001).

Thomas describes /u/ and /ʊ/ fronting as "not... predominant in African American speech..." and notes that "... avoidance of it may have become an identity marker..." for them (2001: 34). Thomas points out, however, that "a few African Americans" show these changes, including five African American speakers in his study of New World Englishes (34). Although sociolinguists tend to characterize /u/ and /ʊ/ fronting as characteristic of White, but not Black speech, recent studies in both urban and rural areas in and out of the South such as Detroit (Anderson *et al.* 2002), Memphis, TN (Fridland 2003), the rural Smoky Mountains of North Carolina (Childs 2005), and rural Hyde County, NC (Wolfram and Thomas 2002), report fronting of /u/, as well as /ʊ/, for African American speakers. Apparently, at least some African Americans in diverse locales are participating in these widespread changes, which are not limited to Whites. More generally, Labov (1994, 2001) suggests that African Americans do not participate in any of the large-scale vowel rotations in American English.

Johnson (2003: 118) describes fronted /u/ as a feature of General American English. However, fronting of /u/ and /ʊ/ is not restricted to American varieties of English. Stockwell and Minkova (1997: 294) point out that fronting of these vowels has also been documented for Southern British English and Australian English. Anderson and Milroy (MS) also discuss this change as being "socially and geographically widespread" and point out that it is well documented not only in American and British varieties of English, but also in New Zealand English (see also MacMahon 1998: 461; Trudgill *et al.* 2000). Fronting of the high and lower-high back vowels appears to be a global phenomenon in English. I will argue in Chapter 8 that the global nature of this change does not make it a good candidate for constituting a crucial site (see Section 2.1.4) for the articulation and negotiation of local identity.

Section 2.1 described work on vowel shifts in American English, including the Northern Cities Shift, the Southern Shift, the high and lower-high back vowels, and /ai/. Internally motivated change (described below) is generally discussed in terms of these shifts in work on American English vowel systems, and the AAE system is usually dismissed in this literature as not affected by them.

2.2 Models of change

2.2.1 Internal and external factors in language change

Language change is often described as resulting from internal factors (Labov 1994), from external factors (Labov 2001), or from a combination of internal and external factors (Fridland 2003; Watt 2000, among others). Campbell (1999: 286) describes internal "causes" of change as " . . . based on what human speech production and perception is and is not capable of . . . Internal causes include both physical and psychological factors. . . . " Campbell describes external causes of change as arising from " . . . largely outside the structure of language itself and outside the human organism . . . " and including "expressive uses of languages . . . " (287). Anderson and Milroy (MS) note that variationist research seldom attempts to integrate socially motivated and intrasystemic factors in accounts of language change.

Labov analyzes internal factors (1994) and social factors (2001) separately, and describes the interface between language and society as "narrow." He further comments on the "relative segregation of social and structural elements in language" (2001: 29). Labov, then, views the interaction of internal and external factors as limited. Labov (1994) argues that large-scale vowel rotations of the kind discussed in Section 2.1 are structured by language-internal principles. He postulates a set of principles based on a survey of a large number of chain shifts. The thrust of his proposal is that chain shifts result from vowel systems' tendency to preserve symmetry (1994: 115–54).

I will suggest in Chapter 8 that, rather labeling some changes as internal and others as external, a given change should be examined in terms of internal constraints and external motivations. In other words, the interplay between internal and external factors is important to consider in investigations of change. Specifically, after discussing the question of which aspects of vowel changes reported in Chapters 6 and 7 are susceptible to being ideologized and which, if any, are not, I will argue that some types of vowel changes (such as /ai/ glide-reduction) provide a crucial site for linguistically indexing social oppositions, while others (such as the fronting of /u/ and /ʊ/) do not. In this view, there is no dichotomy between "internal" and "external" types of changes such as those proposed by Labov (1994, 2001). Instead, I specify how each vowel change is shaped by both internal and external factors; underpinning this view is an assumption that vowel realizations need to be treated multidimensionally as physical, cognitive, and social. Specifically, we shall see in Chapters 6 and 7 that the fronting of /u/ and /ʊ/ is contextually constrained while /ai/ glide-weakening is not. In Chapter 8, I advocate an approach that is sensitive to the influences of coarticulation on sound change and argue that vowel changes are internally constrained but subject to ideological intervention. Context effects, in this case, coarticulation with the following consonant, are examples of internal constraints on changes which are also, depending on the social context, subject to ideological intervention.

Section 2.2.3 describes a language ideological framework developed by linguistic anthropologists, which I will make reference to in the interpretation and conclusions given in Chapter 8.

2.2.2   Language ideology: An overview

Silverstein (1992, 1996), Woolard and Schieffelin (1994), Kroskrity (2000), Irvine and Gal (2000), and others treat language ideologies as conceptual schemes that are used to interpret and understand language variation. Irvine and Gal (2000: 35) characterize these conceptual schemes as ideological because "they are suffused with the political and moral issues pervading the particular sociolinguistic field and are subject to the interests of their bearers' social position." Woolard (1998: 3) describes language ideology as "representations, whether explicit or implicit, that construe the intersection of language and human beings in a social world . . . " and as " . . . a mediating link between social forms and forms of talk. . . . " Silverstein (1979: 193) defines language ideology as " . . . sets of beliefs about language articulated by users as a rationalization or justification of perceived language structure or use." Kroskrity (2000: 21) explicitly comments on the connection of language ideology with speakers:

> Language users' ideologies bridge their sociocultural experience and their linguistic and discursive resources by constituting those linguistic and discursive forms as indexically tied to features of their sociocultural experience. These users, in constructing language ideologies, are selective both in the features of linguistic and social systems that they do distinguish and the linkages between systems that they construct.

In short, language ideologies are beliefs about language and interpretations of its relationships with its social and cultural setting. Language itself, as well as beliefs about it, is viewed as inherently socially and culturally positioned. Analyses of the group of scholars discussed above address and refine the role of social identity in structuring language change. The situation of AAE and Appalachian English in Detroit is well suited to an analysis in a language ideological framework which addresses and integrates the roles of social structure and of speaker attitudes in shaping the direction of language change. Irvine and Gal (2000: 47) revisit Labov's (1963) study of Martha's Vineyard to show how such an analysis might work:

> Contrasts among ethnic groups of islanders (Yankees, Portuguese, and Indians) in the 1930s were replaced by a contrast between islanders and mainlanders in the 1960s. Islander phonology diverged ever more sharply from mainland forms after the development of the tourist industry made that contrast more socially significant than local, intra-island differences. Although Labov did not explore the content of language ideology giving rise to these changes, the case seems to beg for just this type of analysis and illustrates language change as an ideologically fueled process of increasing divergence. We can call the divergence ideologically mediated because it depended on local images of salient social categories that shifted over time.

In Chapter 8, I will argue that "local images of salient social categories that (shift) over time" (Irvine and Gal 2000: 47) are important to consider in the analysis of the vowel changes reported for the Southern migrant participants in Chapters 6 and 7.

Language ideologies are manifested not only in reactions and attitudes to varieties (like AAE) or linguistic forms (such as /ai/ glide-weakening or high and lower-high back vowel fronting) used by salient social groups (such as Southern migrants), but in patterns of language use. Anderson and Milroy (MS) note that this extension of the scope of ideological analysis from language attitudes to include patterns of use distinguishes the approach of Irvine, Gal, and their colleagues from most sociolinguistic work on language ideologies (Lippi-Green 1997, for example). Anderson and Milroy (MS) suggest that ideologies change as "... particular groups shift in and out of salience in the sociolinguistic landscape at different times and places." Changing ideologies can yield different patterns of use and are thus an important component of processes of language change.

2.2.3 Dialect contact

The dialect contact framework specified by Trudgill (1986) adds an important dimension to the discussion of the dynamics driving language change in the aftermath of speaker mobility and migration, and I shall make reference to it in Chapter 8. Labov's approach to phonological change does not examine the effects of dialect contact (Labov 2001: 20).

Thomason (2001: 62) defines contact-induced change as "... any linguistic change that would have been less likely to occur outside a particular contact situation...." In her discussion of linguistic "predictors" of contact-induced change, Thomason notes that "speakers' attitudes can and sometimes do produce exceptions to...most...generalizations..." (2001: 77). In this regard, she points out, language change is unpredictable: "even the most 'natural' structural changes—common changes that occur frequently in diverse languages all over the world—often do not happen" (77). Thomason's view of speaker attitudes disrupting or redirecting contact-induced change suggests that there is an interplay of some sort between internal and external factors in language change. One goal of this study is to specify the interaction between internal and external factors for the vowel changes described in Chapters 6 and 7.

One frequently occurring process which is the result of language contact in the aftermath of migration and mobility is dialect leveling, a process which involves the eradication of variants within and also between systems (Trudgill 1986: 98). Leveling is likely to occur following large-scale migrations such as those of the African American and Appalachian Southern migrants in this study. Chapter 8 discusses a change in Detroit AAE in terms of allophonic leveling.

This chapter described the empirical and theoretical background to the study, focusing respectively on American English vowel shifts in progress and socially oriented models of language change. Chapter 3 turns to the sociolinguistic setting of the research.

3
The Sociolinguistic and Demographic Context for the Study

This chapter describes the research site of the study. It also discusses the migration history of African American and Appalachian White migrants to Detroit as well as the relationship between these two groups. I also discuss work on the phonological characteristics of the three varieties involved in this language contact situation. Research on Appalachian English and AAE, both in the South and in Southeastern Michigan, is reviewed along with work on Midwestern White vowel systems in the Detroit area.

3.1 Research site and demography of the area

African American and Southern White migrant groups migrated from the South to Detroit at about the same time and for similar economic reasons (discussed in Section 3.2). This shared history and subsequent contact raise a number of interrelated issues concerning the extent to which the two groups share phonological systems associated with the South, their level of participation (if any) in the socially and geographically pervasive series of vowel rotations known as the Northern Cities Shift (NCS), and possible interacting effects of ethnicity, regional affiliation, and dialect contact on patterns of language use.

One difference in the histories of the two groups is that eventually many of the Appalachian Whites were able to immerse themselves in the general White population, moving out of the city and into "blue collar" inner suburbs (Sugrue 1996: 246). In contrast, while there are some African Americans in the suburbs, the city of Detroit is overwhelmingly populated by African Americans (U.S. Census 2000). Detroit has a long history of violent racial conflicts (Farley *et al.* 2000). Farley *et al.* (2000) describe Detroit as an extremely segregated metropolis, an area divided primarily along White and Black racial lines. Figure 3.1 shows the metropolitan Detroit area by percentage of African American residents. The 2000 Census figures for the city of Detroit show that it is 82% African American and 12% White. The inner suburbs, in stark contrast, are predominately White. Relevant

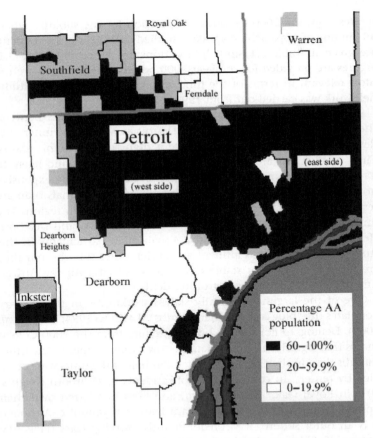

Figure 3.1 The location of fieldwork sites (adapted from a map provided by Wayne State University Center for Urban Studies, http://www.cus.wayne.edu/)

Table 3.1 Figures of 2000 census for White and African American residents for the Appalachian fieldwork sites

Inner suburb	White (%)	African American (%)
Dearborn Heights	92	2
Royal Oak	95	2
Warren	91	3
Taylor	86	9

figures from the 2000 Census of Population for the suburbs, where all but one of Appalachian speakers studied in this study are resident, are given in Table 3.1, and the locations are shown in Figure 3.1. Figures are provided for the year 2000 because these figures are the most relevant in terms of the time of data collection for the study; fieldwork was carried out from 1999 to 2002.

SEMCOG (1994) describes the demographic differences between the outer and the inner suburbs of Detroit as well as the inner city. Residents of the outer suburbs have a high socioeconomic status. Their populations are predominantly White, wealthy, and likely to have extensive formal education. These residents occupy expensive homes, are mobile, and are more likely to be professionals than are residents in any other part of the Detroit metropolitan region. The inner suburbs, including Warren, Taylor, Royal Oak, and Dearborn Heights (where all but one of the Appalachian participants in this study reside), are not as affluent as the rich outer suburbs, but they are more economically stable than the inner city. All the African American participants are Detroit residents.

One of the largest technically skilled workforces in the country populates the "blue collar" inner suburbs (SEMCOG 1994; Farley *et al.* 2000). Demographic data for housing tenure from the 2000 Census shows that significantly more families own their homes in the inner suburbs than in the city. In Detroit about half of the units were occupied by renters. In contrast, 85% of residents in Dearborn Heights, 70% in Royal Oak, 71% in Taylor, and 80% in Warren own their homes. The Detroit White participant lives in Wyandotte. Although it is an outer suburb, it is predominantly working class (Elias MS; Frekko MS; SEMCOG 1994). The 2000 Census data show that 73% of Wyandotte residents own their homes.

3.2 History of migration to southeastern Michigan

Large numbers of Southerners migrated to southeastern Michigan in the early decades of the twentieth century to work in factories which offered higher wages than could be found in the South, which was still largely agrarian. The Great Southern Migration began during World War I and continued unabated through the 1960s (Sugrue 1996). Recognizing the magnitude of this migration from the South, commentators have called Detroit a "magnet" for African American and White Southern migrants (Sugrue 1996: 12, 212).

3.2.1 Appalachian White migration to Detroit

Southern Highlanders migrated to Detroit in large numbers (Hartigan 1999; Berry 2000) from the Appalachian Mountains of West Virginia, Kentucky, Tennessee, and North Carolina, a region that was historically isolated from the rest of the South. The economic picture of the rural South was (and is) grim. Farmers with small acreage and subsistence farmers grew increasingly marginalized from mainstream industrialized America in the last three decades of the nineteenth century, and industrial capitalism's rise was ". . . inversely related to subsistence agriculture's demise" (Berry 2000: 15). Historian Chad Berry, the grandson of Southern migrants, describes the importance of kinship ties in the migration process: ". . . the highways that led northward were built on kinship, a factor that often determined where a migrant went as well as where he or she lived. . . (and) worked" (Berry 2000: 6–7). The urban Midwest offered economic incentives to migrants, but the South was home to important cultural values such as those of homeland, family, community, and religious affiliation.

Appalachian migrants began arriving in Detroit as early as World War I (Berry 2000: 12). Elmer Akers was one early writer who investigated early Southern migrants to the Detroit area, and he describes the difficulties they encountered:

> (the) characteristic of mind and personality, combined with a pitifully meager education and almost total unfamiliarity with the ways and demands of a high-speed industrial society makes their difficulties of accommodation to Detroit almost insuperably great. (Akers 1936: 7)

Akers conducted interviews with businessmen, employment agency representatives, landlords, and grocers in Detroit and with Southern migrants themselves. His main observation is that Southern Whites do not assimilate to Northern culture or lifestyles and as a result they face considerable hostility in securing work and locating housing. Several management officials in charge of hiring whom Aker interviewed stated that they did not often hire Southern Whites because of their frequent trips back down South. An official involved in the hiring process at a Detroit auto factory responds thus:

> They are rovers, a transient group of people . . . And they are pretty slow. They have no drive, most of them. They don't establish residence here and try to get ahead. It got so we wouldn't hire them at all, toward the last—toward 1929. I got tired of seeing Southerners. You can tell a Southerner as soon as he opens his mouth, you know, if not by his appearance. I would tell them "I don't want you fellows from the South. You don't stick to your job. The first thing we know you are gone . . . back South". (Akers 1936: 41)

Southern Whites also faced housing discrimination. Many of the landlords who were interviewed in the 1930s stated they did not like to rent to them. One merchant explained to Akers that the Southern Whites "affect(ed) property values and neighborhood qualifications very much as do Negroes" and pointed out that many would not rent to them for this reason (Akers 1936: 14).

Akers (1936) also describes the way Southern White migrants integrated as a distinctive group in Detroit rather than blending into the Midwestern White community:

> Again and again we got the impression that the Southern Whites were in the neighborhood but not of it, in the city but not in any sense a real part of it. Many women we talked with knew no Northern women, and their communal life was entirely a matter of informal associations with other Southern White women. (Akers 1936: 63)

> . . . they are not concerned about what Northerners think of them. Status seemed to be almost wholly a matter of in-group relations among most of those we interviewed. (Akers 1936: 65)

Akers also comments, "Socially the Southern Whites are a self-contained group. This statement is quite as true as it would be of any group of immigrants from a foreign country, if not more so" (Akers 1936: 65).

Early Southern White migrants in Detroit appear to have faced considerable hostility from the general population at the beginning of the migration period. Akers reports that many of the Northern Whites he interviewed stated frankly that they did not like Southern Whites or want them in their neighborhoods or at their places of work (Akers 1936: 73). Given the hostility of Detroit Whites to the arrival of Southern Whites, as well as the importance of strong kinship ties and rural cultural values to these migrants, it is not surprising that they formed and maintained close ties with other Southern Whites in Detroit, even if they did not migrate from the same hill, "holler," or even state. As Berry (2000: 136) points out, this kind of group formation is one of the strongest indicators that Southern White migrants called on their past once in the North and hence demonstrated an important type of minority behavior (see also Stewart 1996).

Although these early migrants faced severe discrimination in employment and housing and were not welcomed by their Northern neighbors, later generations of Southern White migrants appear to have found the Detroit area more hospitable. Between 1945 and 1960, migration from the rural South increased dramatically, resulting in one of the largest internal migrations in U.S. history. Berry (2000: 104) describes four important characteristics of this migration. It occurred not just from Appalachia, but also from nearly all areas of the Upland South. Southern migrants were quite visible in the North due to their massive numbers, unique cultural characteristics, and distinctive dialects. Kinship ties played a crucial role in migration. Berry describes these kinship ties as "very broad, including not only kin but also friends . . . whom they could call . . . and depend on for support once in the North" (120). Berry also reports that Southern migrants began to be more economically successful during the years of 1945–1960.

Several researchers comment on the distinctive cultural characteristics which Southern migrants retained after relocating to the Midwest. Berry (2000: 134) comments, "Even those migrants who were most 'assimilated' never completely ceased to be . . . Southern." He also reports that Southern migrants often formed community and neighborhood clubs in Detroit and showed a significant degree of "cultural retention" of Southern traditions such as the Southern Baptist religion and Bluegrass music.

3.2.2   African American migration to Detroit

African Americans migrated to Detroit primarily from the Deep South and old plantation areas—Alabama, Mississippi, Georgia, South Carolina, and the Piedmont and coastal regions of North Carolina; however, some African American migrants did come from the non-plantation regions of the South, such as the Southern Appalachian mountains and Texas. All the African American participants in this study reported their migration was from the former plantation areas of the South. Sugrue (1996: 23) describes the period between 1916 and 1929 as the "Great Migration" of African Americans to Midwestern industrial centers such as Detroit. This migration continued unabated into the 1950s as more African Americans from the South joined friends and relatives already living in Detroit (30). Like the Appalachian White migration, the African American migration was also predominately kin-based, following a similar pattern of chain migration. Another important similarity shared by Appalachian Whites and African American Southern migrants is that both groups typically migrated from rural areas (Marks 1989; Berry 2000).

Detroit's history of racial conflicts includes two severe riots. The first of these, in which both African Americans and Midwestern Whites participated, occurred in 1943. African American residents also rioted in 1967. There were several factors which contributed to the Detroit riots. African Americans were subject to residential, economic, and social segregation in the Detroit area. Sugrue (1996) describes the residential segregation of African Americans in detail:

> White Detroiters invented communities of race in the city that they defined spatially... Whiteness, and by implication, Black-ness, assumed a material dimension, imposed on the geography of the city (234).

During the period of school desegregation, White neighborhood "civic" groups were formed for the purpose of keeping African American families out of their neighborhoods. These neighborhood groups sprang up throughout many of the suburbs (Sugrue 1996).

Farley *et al.* (2000), cited in Anderson and Milroy (MS), also describe the historical and current residential segregation of African Americans in Detroit.

> Following the urban riots of the 1960s [in Detroit], the Kerner Commission bleakly described what they thought the future held if the government failed to address the nation's fundamental racial inequalities: a nation divided into largely black and impoverished central cities surrounded by largely white and prosperous suburban rings. . . . They were wrong about New York, Los Angeles, Washington and other locations, since immigration from Asia and Latin America changed the composition of many central cities. And the Kerner Commission did not foresee the substantial shift of African Americans to the suburbs that began in the 1980s. But they were right about Detroit: economic changes since 1970, combined with continuing racial polarization and the longstanding movement of Whites—but not Blacks—to the suburbs, make Detroit the polarized metropolis they predicted. (Farley *et al.* 2000: 51–52)

Why has the segregation of African Americans persisted so long in Detroit? Farley *et al.*'s (2000) large-scale sociological survey of Detroit, which investigated employer hiring practices and attitudes toward the integration of African Americans into White neighborhoods, showed that many Whites in the Detroit area still hold negative stereotypes about African Americans:

> Despite strong endorsement of the ideals of equal treatment for all races, the remnants of traditional racial stereotypes are still present in the thinking of many Detroit area Whites. The majority endorses the idea that Blacks are not easy to get along with and prefer more than Whites to live on welfare. (245)

Sugrue (1996), Farley *et al.* (2000), and SEMCOG (1994) all conclude that Detroit African Americans typically have worse jobs, lower incomes, and poorer housing than Whites and predominantly live in the city rather than the suburbs.

This section demonstrates that there are important similarities in the migration histories of Appalachian White and African American Southern groups and the discrimination they encountered in Detroit.

Section 3.3 describes reports by a number of researchers on the relations between these migrant groups in the Detroit area.

3.3   Appalachian Whites and African American Southern migrants in the Detroit area

In addition to the commonalities described in Sections 3.2.1 and 3.2.2, the evidence reviewed in this section suggests that African American and Appalachian White Southern migrants and their descendants share a number of important cultural characteristics with each other. Edwards (1997) reports that Detroit African Americans frequently visit relatives in the South, and Berry's (2000) analysis of oral history among White migrants shows the same pattern of frequent and extended visits with friends and family in the South. Recall also that both the African American and Appalachian White migrations from the South to Detroit were largely kin-based. As discussed below, White and Black Southern migrants lived in close proximity to each other, at least through the 1950s and 1960s. In contrast, as already discussed in Section 3.2, Northern Whites were extremely resistant to African Americans moving into their neighborhoods.

Akers (1936) provides excerpts of interviews he conducted with White Southern migrants in Detroit which suggest that even these early White migrants may have been accommodating of African Americans. For example, Akers asked one Southern family what they disliked about Detroit. A high-school-age boy, seconded by his parents, said:

> the people up here think we don't like it because the Negroes are given equal rights with White people. But I don't think that's so . . . What we don't like is that you northerners seem to think the foreigners have more right to work and to a place here than the Southerners do. (74)

Akers attributes such attitudes to non-Americans having achieved a more secure and more prosperous niche in the city's industrial and social economy than either African Americans or White Southerners.

A more recent account of relations between Southern Whites and African Americans is provided by the anthropologist John Hartigan, who conducted ethnographic fieldwork among Southern Whites in the Briggs and Corktown communities on the Southwest side of Detroit from July 1992 through February 1994. He reports that Whites in these neighborhoods never assimilated into mainstream Midwestern White culture, and describes close relationships between these Southern Whites and Blacks. Hartigan also comments on the importance of class in the construction of White racial identity:

> The clarity of the category (hillbilly) primarily stands out in relation to the degree of assimilation into mainstream White middle class . . . culture. The term's primary contrast inscribed the difference between Whites who assimilated successfully in this northern industrial town and those who retained behaviors or lived in conditions that were somehow improper for Whites. It seemed to me that it was the hillbillies' very close proximity to Blacks that often heightened this sense of impropriety. (Hartigan 1999: 89–90)

In addition to describing close relationships with African Americans, some participants in Hartigan's study also described the 1967 riot in regional rather than racial terms. One native-born Northern White woman comments on how this riot marked the culmination of two decades of White and Black Southern migration which "forever transformed" her neighborhood:

> you had Northern people acting like they (the Southerners) were invading their territory; they were up in arms, and they fought each other. But there are more Southerners here now than there is anything else. That's because the Northerners just went further north (after the riot). (Hartigan 1999: 49–50)

Hartigan concludes that Southern Whites and African Americans in his fieldwork sites treat each other as individuals and react in terms of occupational, social, cultural, and regional characteristics rather than in terms of race.

Berry (2000) reports that when he asked Southern Whites what they disliked most about Detroit they frequently mentioned Northern Whites but, significantly, never African Americans. Hartigan asked his participants the same question. One participant who had retired from the workforce responds thus:

> Most of the hillbillies do not like Yankees to start with. We were true Southerners even though we worked in Detroit. We still had to stick together even though we lived in Yankeeland and worked for Yankees. We didn't like Yankees. That's our heritage. (Hartigan 1999: 139–140)

Both African American and Appalachian Southern White migrants brought a Southern rural culture to Detroit which was discordant with the Northern urban culture.

Unlike the inner city participants in Hartigan's study, the majority of Southern migrants in the greater Detroit area, according to Sugrue (1996), did not remain in inner city enclaves but rather dissolved into the suburban landscape:

> Hillbillies, as they were labeled, were frequently blamed for racial tension in the city, but their role was greatly exaggerated. Most of them dispersed throughout the metropolitan area, and quickly disappeared into the larger White population. (Sugrue 1996: 212)

Berry (2000) also comments on the eventual economic success of many Southern White migrants. However, Berry argues that these migrants nevertheless show a great deal of "cultural retention" of rural, Southern cultural traditions (Berry 2000: 136).

This section discussed the shared cultural and regional orientation of White and African American Detroit Southern migrants. Although the groups have much in common in these respects, African Americans, unlike Southern Whites, have never been able to immerse themselves into the general White suburban population, no matter what their socioeconomic status is.

The next section discusses sociophonetic work on the varieties of English spoken by the two groups in the context of Appalachian and African American varieties of English in the South and local Midwestern White vowel norms.

3.4   Appalachian English

3.4.1   In the Southern Highlands

Appalachian English in the Southern Highlands, an area which stretches along the Appalachian mountain range from West Virginia to Northern Georgia in the American South, is relatively under-researched. As Hazen and Fluharty (2001) stress, there is more than one variety of English spoken in a region which spans portions of six states. The vowel rotation traditionally cited as characteristic of the dialects of the Southern Highlands, the Southern Shift, was described in Section 2.1.2.

Wolfram and Christian (1976) investigated Appalachian English in Mercer and Monroe counties in West Virginia. With respect to phonological variation, they focus mainly on consonantal features such as consonant cluster reduction (CCR), intrusive *t* in clusters like *oncet* for "once," and /l/ deletion *hep* for "help." They also discuss unstressed syllable deletion *maters* for "tomatoes." For vowels, they describe glide-reduction for /ai/ and the pre-nasal merger of [ɪ] and [ɛ]. Although consonant features are certainly important in describing the phonological patterns of any variety, this study will focus on portions of the vowel system which are implicated in the Southern Shift.

Anderson (1998, 1999) investigated /e/, /o/, /ai/, and /oi/ in Appalachian English in Graham County, North Carolina, in the heart of the Great Smoky Mountains. The results of that acoustic study showed that all 30 White participants adopted realizations of /e/ and /o/ which follow the pattern for the Southern Shift described in Section 2.1.2. /oi/ showed a low, back nucleus and glide toward the high front portion of the vowel space. /ai/ is discussed further below.

Hazen and Fluharty (2001) found that "traditional" Appalachian dialect features, including /ai/ monophthongization and ungliding, were dying out among young West Virginians, but it is important to note that many of their speakers are suburban rather than rural, and several of them are what these researchers call "first-generation" Appalachians since they have in fact moved to the Appalachian region from the North. Here I treat the designation "Appalachian" as an ethnic category (see further Hartigan 1999; Stewart 1996), rather than as a designation for people who simply live in a given area (such as Northerners who live among ethnic Appalachian populations). It is the traditional Appalachian features which are of relevance to this study, rather than the modern leveled suburban dialect described by Hazen and Fluharty.

I will discuss /ai/ in detail here because it is an important marker of regional identity in the South. Hall (1942: 43) describes a pattern of glide-weakening for his data from the Smoky Mountains of North Carolina, indicating that /ai/ is most often realized as [a:] in all phonetic environments. In fact, he notes that the tendency in general Southern American speech at that time was to monophthongize /ai/ in voiced environments, such as *ride* [ra:d], but to retain the diphthong in voiceless environments, such as in *light* [lait]. This pattern did not, however, hold true for Highland Southern English in the Smoky Mountains, where a glide-weakened variant, [a:], was preferred in all phonetic environments (Hall 1942: 43). Kurath and McDavid (1961) found evidence of glide-weakening for the word *twice* in Western North Carolina and for the words *nine* and *might* in Macon County, which borders Graham County. The data for the word *might* provided by the LAMSAS office at the University of Georgia indicates that /ai/ was nearly monophthongal in Western North Carolina in both pre-voiced and pre-voiceless environments in the 1930s and that diphthongal pre-voiceless /ai/ was already a relic form in this area. Wolfram and Christian (1976: 64) found that Appalachian English speakers in their study of two counties in West Virginia participated in the glide-reduction of /ai/, and they determined the order, from most to least favorable, for following phonetic environments for this feature to be pause > voiced obstruent > voiceless obstruent. This ordering falls in line with the traditional constraint pattern for general Southern American English and is in contrast to Hall's (1942) observation that the /ai/ glide was reduced in all following phonetic environments in the Smoky Mountain region of Western North Carolina.

Williams (1992: 14) also describes /ai/ in Appalachian English as glide-weakened, and although he cites the classic example of the general Southern American pronunciation of [a:s] for *ice*, he does not discuss the effect of following phonetic environment on the patterning of the variable. Pederson (1983: 73) indicates that /ai/ for seventy East Tennessean informants is realized most often as a monophthong and, less frequently, as a short diphthong. He further notes that /ai/ is typically monophthongal before voiceless consonants, as in *write* or *light*, for all age and social groups of the region (75).

Acoustic data for /ai/ for Whites in Graham County, North Carolina, presents a similar picture of present-day Smoky Mountain English, which is largely glide-reduced for /ai/ in all following phonetic environments (Anderson 1997, 1998, 1999). In fact, all the 30 White participants in that project showed categorically weakened variants in all phonetic environments.

In summary, with the exception of the work of Wolfram and Christian (1976) and Hazen and Fluharty (2001) in West Virginia, researchers have found a pattern of glide-reduction for /ai/ in all phonetic contexts in Appalachia, including the salient pre-voiceless environment. This important pattern, a relatively recent development in the lowland South but a change at completion in some varieties of Appalachian English, is relevant to the discussion of the acoustic analysis of /ai/ presented in Chapter 7.

The next section discusses sociolinguistic work on the dialects of Appalachian migrants and their descendants in Ypsilanti, Michigan, a town about 30 miles to the west of Detroit.

3.4.2 In Southeastern Michigan

Evans *et al.* (2000) and Evans (2001) investigated /æ/-raising, an NCS feature, among Appalachian descendants in Ypsilanti, Michigan. They found that Ypsilanti Appalachian speakers adopted the local raised pronunciation for this vowel, leading Evans (2001) to conclude that the descendants of Appalachian migrants in Ypsilanti acquired a new Midwestern identity at the expense of their previously regionally based Southern Appalachian identity. In contrast, the results of my own work show that the Detroit area Appalachian participants retain and maintain both regional Appalachian speech patterns and a social and cultural orientation to the Southern Highlands (see Chapters 4 and 8). It is unclear why Appalachian Whites in Detroit would show less accommodation to Midwestern White linguistic norms than Appalachian Whites in Ypsilanti.

Next I turn to descriptions of AAE, both in the South and in the urban Midwest.

3.5 African American English

Descriptions by researchers of AAE vowel systems were reviewed in Section 2.1.3. This section considers reports on AAE in the Southern United States and in the Detroit and Lansing areas of Michigan.

3.5.1 In the South

According to Labov (1994), African Americans do not participate in the changes associated with the Southern Shift. Likewise, Thomas concludes that "in general the African American avoidance of sound changes that have occurred in White vernaculars holds true in the South" (2001: 170). However, there are reports that AAE speakers do participate in some sound changes traditionally described as characteristic of White varieties. For example, Fridland (2001) found that her entire all-female sample of AAE speakers in Memphis, TN, showed evidence of the Southern Shift (see Section 2.1.2 for a description of the Southern Shift). They showed reversal for /e/ and /ɛ/ and the fronting of /u/. Fridland concludes that the Southern Shift is better characterized as regionally based than as ethnically based, contrary to Labov's (1991, 1994) treatment of this series of vowel changes (see Section 2.1.2). Wolfram (2007) cautions against treating AAE as a homogeneous trans-regional variety.

3.5.2 In Southeastern Michigan

Edwards (1997) investigated the persistence of Southern features in Detroit speech. He noted that /ai/ was monophthongized for the African American participants in his study but did not distinguish it by different following phonetic contexts in his analysis. He described monophthongal [a:] as an important feature of group identity for working-class speakers in his study.

Detroit AAE has also been examined with regard to presence or absence of features associated with the NCS. Deser (1990) analyzed the vowel systems of 18 speakers from the Shuy *et al.*'s (1968) sample. She attempted to determine whether these speakers showed /æ/-raising but was unable to discern clear patterns (Deser 1990: 109). Gordon (2001: 91) points out that it is difficult to draw conclusions from Deser's results. For example, Deser makes the claim that younger speakers' productions are more "Northern-like" than those of teenagers and adults, but her sample is skewed by the fact that several of these speakers' families are not in fact Southern migrants. Rather, they were already resident in Detroit prior to the Great Black Migration from the rural South. Deser also noted, however, that children with Southern African American parents appeared to monophthongize /ai/, producing in some cases 100% monophthongization. I will return to this important observation in Chapter 8.

Jones (MS) investigated the speech of African Americans in Lansing, Michigan, a city 55 miles northwest of Detroit, and found evidence of recent Southern sound changes. She reports that older speakers in her sample show fronting for /u/ and /ʊ/ along with lowering of /e/, all of these being Southern Shift features. In contrast, Jones reports minimal evidence for two women of an NCS feature, fronting for /ɑ/, and concludes that her results "may indicate a conservative trend among Northern AAE speakers or a reaffirmation of the group's Southern identity" (24).

Jones and Preston (in press) investigated pre-oral /æ/-raising and /ɑ/-fronting among African American females in Lansing. They found that eight out of nine speakers showed raising for /æ/, but they found no fronting for /ɑ/. They conclude that /æ/-raising is a local linguistic norm which "... has nothing to do with the African American identity of Lansing speakers..." (16). They note further that "it seems that AAE speakers may choose to adopt and adapt certain local features, which may grant them a regional label..., yet they also possess strictly AAE features... "(32). Interestingly, the patterns reported by Jones and Preston for African Americans in Lansing are quite different for those which will be reported in later chapters for Detroit African Americans. It seems that Lansing and Detroit differ with respect to the assimilation of African Americans to Midwestern White vowel norms.

3.6 Midwestern urban Whites

As discussed in Section 2.1.1, the NCS is a series of vowel changes reported to be in operation in the Midwest, particularly in the urban centers. Eckert (1987, 1988, 1989, 1991, 2000) investigated the NCS in two Detroit suburbs, engaging in two years of participant obser-vation in two high schools. Eckert (2000) found that the older NCS changes (the raising of /æ/ and fronting of /ɑ/) correlated only with gender, with the girls leading in the use of advanced variants. Eckert (2000) also reported patterns for /ai/, which is socially salient in Detroit. Although Eckert found some /ai/ monophthongization among adolescent boys, it did not occur before pre-voiceless consonants. Eckert found that this context strongly favored the raising and backing of the /ai/ nucleus, i.e. [ʌi]; this realization of /ai/ showed no social stratification among the White teenagers in Eckert's study, but it indexes a very sharp distinction with Detroit African Americans. In fact, Eckert (2000: 136) characterized /ai/ raising and backing as a "newer variable" which is more advanced in areas closer to the urban center. This feature, also called "Canadian raising," is widespread in the Midwest. I will return to this point in Chapter 8.

Popular attitudes toward local varieties of English are also relevant to this study. Niedzielski (1999: 80–81) reports that White speakers in Detroit report that they are speakers of "standard" speech. Based on the results of their extensive sociological surveys, Farley *et al.* (2000: 223) describe the same attitude: "Among Whites in Metro Detroit (the city plus the inner suburbs) there is still a widespread belief that Whites speak the (English) language better than Blacks." Such language ideologies are important to my analysis in Chapter 8.

This chapter discussed the research sites where data for this study was collected and described the migration histories and cultural orientations of Detroit Appalachian White and African American Southern migrants. It also reviewed the relevant sociolinguistic work on Appalachian English, AAE, and Detroit suburban White varieties.

4

The Pilot Study

A three-year pilot study informed the design of the study reported in Chapters 5, 6, and 7. The pilot analyzes /ai/ for 27 Detroit AAE speakers (Section 4.1). In addition, the patterning of /ɛ/ and /æ/ is described in Section 4.2 for five of the Detroit AAE speakers, five Detroit Appalachian English speakers, and five Midwestern Whites (Anderson and Milroy 2001a,b; Anderson 2002). I conducted ethnographic interviews (described in Section 5.1) with 20 of the African American speakers and 2 of the Appalachian White speakers. Data for the seven additional African Americans comes from a corpus of conversations between Detroit inner city African American mothers and their children, provided by speech pathologists Holly Craig and Julie Washington at the University of Michigan. Data from three additional Appalachian White and all of the Midwestern White speakers was collected by Susan Frekko, a linguistic anthropology graduate student at the University of Michigan. The research site for this study was described in detail in Chapter 3. Data collection procedures are those used in the main study, and are discussed in Section 5.2.

4.1 /ai/

4.1.1 Participants and methods of analysis for the pilot study

Data from 27 AAE speakers were collected by two different interviewers, an African American speech-language pathologist and myself. The speakers were 3 older adults (a man aged 81 and two women aged 70 and 62), 16 younger adults (14 women with an age range of 20–45 and 2 men, aged 42 and 25), and 4 girls and 4 boys aged 4–7. As noted above, I conducted interviews with all of the adults and one of the girls. Data from the other seven children was extracted from the corpus provided by speech pathologists Craig and Washington. This corpus contains spontaneous conversation between Detroit African American mothers and their children and was collected in 1995 for the purpose of assessing dialect acquisition of AAE. Because the patterns reported below are consistent between my interviews and the corpus, it is unlikely that they were due to radical interviewer effect. Although this is not a sample organized systematically by age and gender, the data from both sources together cover a wide age range.

The sociolinguistic interviews I conducted lasted about 60–70 minutes, and the conversations collected by the speech-language pathologist lasted 45–60 minutes. The interviews that I conducted were organized around the talk of participants on the topic of life in contemporary Detroit. My own Southern origins and vernacular Appalachian dialect were helpful in gaining access to the community, and I developed close ties with several key participants. All of these interviews were conducted in participants' homes in the West Side of Detroit and recorded using a Sony portable minidisk recorder (model MZ-R30) and a Sony microphone (model ECM-MS957). Tokens of /ai/ were analyzed impressionistically for presence or absence of a full diphthong. Following Eckert (2001), non-diphthongal tokens were categorized as monophthongal and showed a fronted nucleus and either no glide or a very weak glide. This categorical distinction between diphthongal and monophthongal /ai/ is a limitation of the pilot study that will be addressed in Chapter 7, where I treat "monophthongized" variants gradiently as glide-weakened.

4.1.2 The patterning of /ai/

The results of the impressionistic analysis of /ai/ show that the canonical AAE pattern of diphthongization in pre-voiceless contexts (see Section 2.1.4) emerges in the systems of the three elderly speakers. Figure 4.1 shows that /ai/ monophthongization in the crucial pre-voiceless context is rare for the two older women, and does not occur for the older man. However, the monophthongized variant reported as characteristic of some White varieties of Southern English has spread to pre-voiceless obstruent contexts for the younger adults and children. A robust pattern of distribution is shown in Figure 4.1, in that speakers under 45 years of age contrast with older African Americans

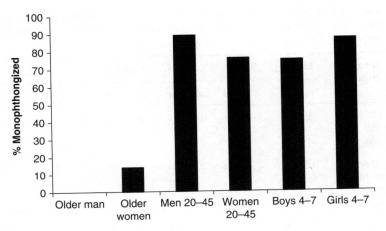

Figure 4.1 Pre-voiceless /ai/ monophthongization by age and gender for 27 Detroit AAE speakers (token *n* = 483) (Anderson 2002)

in using the monophthongized variant at a high level (between 75% and 89%). The distribution of both diphthongized and monophthongized variants for all speakers in a range of phonetic contexts (the input for Figures 4.1 and 4.2) is shown in detail in Table 4.1.

Figure 4.2 shows the percentage of monophthongized variants for all speakers by phonetic environment. Before word-final glottalized

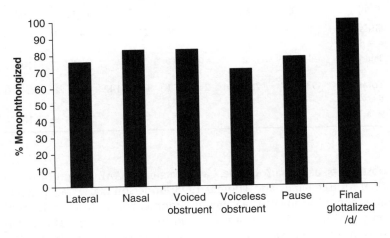

Figure 4.2 AAE /ai/ monophthongization by following environment for 27 Detroit AAE speakers (token *n* = 1241) (Anderson 2002)

Table 4.1 Number and % of [a:] versus [ai] realizations of /ai/ by following phonetic environment. Speakers are grouped by age and gender (Anderson 2002)

Speaker groups	Liquid		Nasal		Vd. Obs.		Vl. Obs.		#		__d#	
	a:	ai	a:	ai	a:	ai	a:	ai	a:	ai	a:	ai
Older man *n* = 1	1	0	17	0	18	3	0	14	5	2		
%[a:]	[100]		100		86		0		71		N/A	
Older women *n* = 2	13	1	21	11	27	11	6	38	9	6	8	0
%[a:]	92		67		71		14		60		100	
Men 20–45 *n* = 2	17	0	27	1	46	4	67	8	17	1	12	0
%[a:]	100		96		92		89		94		100	
Women 20–45 *n* = 14	20	15	95	18	135	24	202	65	52	14	26	0
%[a:]	57		84		85		76		79		100	
Boys 4–7 *n* = 4	1	1	8	1	10	1	39	13	11	2	4	0
%[a:]	[50]		89		91		75		85		100	
Girls 4–7 *n* = 4	1	0	7	5	12	8	27	4	4	3	2	0
%[a:]	[100]		58		60		87		57		[100]	
Total *n* = 27	53	17	175	36	248	51	341	142	98	28	52	0
%[a:]	76		83		83		71		78		100	

obstruents, as in [sa:ʔd] "side," a characteristic AAE variant of word-final /d/ (see Bailey and Thomas 1998; Anderson 2001), /ai/ is typically monophthongal. The other environments vary from each other only slightly, and levels of use are all in excess of 70%. This distribution, together with the age-related pattern shown in Figure 4.1,

Table 4.2 Comparison of Detroit AAE with other varieties for monophthongal realizations of pre-voiceless /ai/

	Pre-voiced [a:]	Pre-voiceless [a:]
Detroit AAE	Yes (Anderson 2002)	Yes (Anderson 2002)
Southern Appalachian White	Yes (Anderson 1999; Thomas 2001)	Yes (Anderson 1999; Thomas 2001)
Southern White varieties in the former plantation regions of the South	Yes (Thomas 2001; Wolfram and Thomas 2002, and others)	Traditional pattern; no progressive varieties; yes (Thomas 2001)
AAE in the South	Yes (Thomas 2001; Wolfram and Thomas 2002; Childs 2005, and others)	AAE in Texana (Childs 2005); incipient fronting in Memphis (Fridland 2004); Hyde County (Wolfram and Thomas 2002)
Northern White	No	No

suggests that the spread of [a:] to the pre-voiceless context is a change in progress close to completion in Detroit AAE.

In summary, the data presented in Figure 4.2 show that the younger speakers in this sample contrast sharply with older speakers in their use of glide-reduced variants of /ai/ in the pre-voiceless obstruent context. Wolfram's work in Detroit suggests that this change started within the last 30 years or so, since /ai/ was diphthongal in this context for African American Detroiters in the sixties (Nguyen 2006), as in AAE generally. Table 4.2 provides a summary of the patterning of /ai/ in relevant varieties.

Although /ai/ was analyzed impressionistically and treated categorically in the pilot study, it will be analyzed acoustically and treated gradiently in the main study.

4.2 Acoustic analysis of /ɛ/ and /æ/ for five Appalachian White women, five African American women, and five Northern White women

The pilot study also investigated the patterning of /ɛ/ and /æ/ in nasal and non-nasal environments for 15 female speakers. /ɛ/ and

/æ/ were chosen because they are part of the Northern Cities Shift (NCS) for Northern Detroit Whites. /ε/ is described as backed and/or lowered for Northern Whites (something like [tʌst] for "test"), and /ae/ is raised ([bɛt] for "bat") (Labov 1994; Wolfram and Schilling-Estes 1998). Nasal and non-nasal environments are compared for the latter vowel because, according to Bailey and Thomas (1998), /æ/-raising occurs before nasals for African American groups generally and is not part of the NCS. They also report that it began in the nineteenth century in AAE, when most African Americans lived in the South. These researchers do not discuss the phonetic factors that condition this change. For /ε/, only pre-obstruent tokens were analyzed.

Participants in this phase of the pilot study include: (i) 2 first-generation and 3 second-/third-generation Appalachian White Southern migrant women, (ii) 2 first-generation and 3 second/third-generation African American Southern migrant women, and (iii) 5 Northern White women (for purposes of comparison). All 15 participants reside in inner Detroit or in its adjacent suburbs. The first-generation speakers are both in their seventies. The second-/third-generation speakers and the Northern White women are in the age range of 30–55 years.

The Praat program was again used for the acoustic analysis. Acoustic measurements of 5–10 tokens of /ε/ and /æ/ for each speaker were taken from casual conversation for the first 3 formants and vowel duration. Formant measurements were taken from fast Fourier transform (FFT) spectra centered at vowel midpoint of each vowel token using a 25-ms Gaussian window and were corroborated by 10-pole linear predictive coding (LPC) spectra (autocorrelation). Normalization of formant values is a controversial procedure (Johnson 1989) that arguably allows one to compare the vowel qualities of speakers with substantially differently sized vocal tracts, particularly men versus women and adults versus children. Because all the speakers discussed here are adult women, normalization was not deemed necessary, so Figures 4.3–4.7 give unnormalized formant values in Hertz.

Figure 4.3 gives the patterning of /ε/ for thee speaker groups and shows that the Northern Whites cluster toward the bottom right of the vowel space, indicating that their /ε/ is generally lower and back relative to that of the Appalachians and African Americans. Figure 4.4 shows the patterning of pre-oral /æ/. The Northern White participants

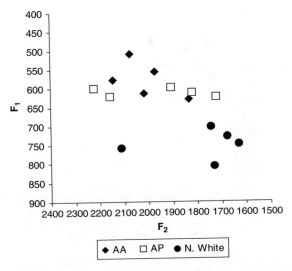

Figure 4.3 The patterning of /ɛ/ for three speaker groups. F_1 and F_2 averages are given in Hz. Each symbol represents the average F_1/F_2 values for each of the five speakers of that group

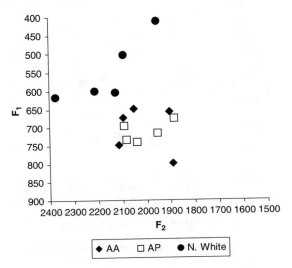

Figure 4.4 The patterning of pre-oral /æ/ for three speaker groups. F_1 and F_2 averages are given in Hz. Each symbol represents the average F_1/F_2 values for each of the five speakers of that group

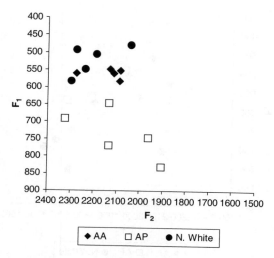

Figure 4.5 The patterning of pre-nasal /æ/ for three speaker groups. F_1 and F_2 averages are given in Hz. Each symbol represents the average F_1/F_2 values for each of the five speakers of that group

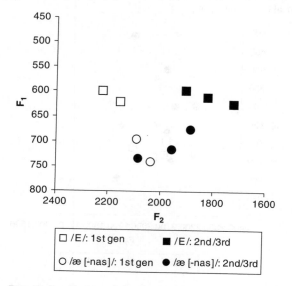

Figure 4.6 Detroit Appalachian /ɛ/ and pre-oral /æ/ by generation. F_1 and F_2 averages are given in Hz. Each symbol represents the average F_1/F_2 values for each of the five speakers of that group

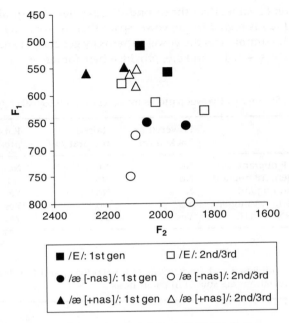

Figure 4.7 Detroit African American /ɛ/, pre-oral /æ/, and pre-nasal /æ/ by generation. F_1 and F_2 averages are given in Hz. Each symbol represents the average F_1/F_2 values for each of the five speakers of that group

have raised /æ/. Comparisons with Figure 4.3 indicate that these speakers' /æ/ (measured at midpoint) is higher and more fronted in the vowel space than their /ɛ/. African American and Appalachian White migrant groups do not show this pattern. Pre-nasal /æ/ is shown in Figure 4.5. Here we see that the African American participants do show raising of pre-nasal /æ/. They cluster directly below the Northern Whites. The Appalachian Whites do not show this pattern of raising of /æ/.

Figure 4.6 gives the F_1/F_2 results for Detroit Appalachian /ɛ/ and /æ/ by generation. First-generation and second-/third-generation speakers do not show differences in raising, though the first-generation speakers generally use more fronted realizations of both vowel qualities. Figure 4.7 is a similar display of the data for the African American participants. The first-generation speakers tend to have lower F_1 values than the second-/third-generation speakers, and pre-nasal /æ/ is higher in the vowel space than pre-oral /æ/.

Table 4.3 summarizes the vowel patterns by generation and speaker group. Tables 4.4, 4.5, and 4.6, provided here for reference, show the

Table 4.3 Summary of vowel patterns by generation and speaker group

	Lowered or backed /ɛ/	Raised pre-oral /æ/	Raised pre-nasal /æ/
1st gen. AP migrant	No	No	No
2nd/3rd gen. AP migrant	No	No	No
1st gen. AA migrant	No	No	Yes
2nd/3rd gen. AA migrant	No	No	Yes
NORTHERN WHITE	Yes	Yes	Yes

Table 4.4 Individual and group averages (in Hz) for F_1 and F_2 values for /ɛ/. Standard deviations are shown in parenthesis

Speaker	F_1		F_2	
	Midpoint	Offset	Midpoint	Offset
AA1	629 (81)	625 (74)	1832 (131)	1726 (132)
AA2	578 (97)	570 (110)	2144 (206)	2098 (245)
AA3	509 (81)	519 (108)	2787 (202)	2069 (194)
AA4	557 (97)	565 (91)	1971 (241)	1855 (165)
AA5	614 (78)	599 (55)	2017 (243)	1930 (215)
AA group	**577 (48)**	**576 (40)**	**2150 (373)**	**1936 (154)**
AP1	611 (54)	602 (67)	1820 (148)	1793 (192)
AP2	621 (76)	553 (113)	2155 (218)	2100 (288)
AP3	597 (57)	582 (49)	1905 (145)	1924 (186)
AP4	599 (57)	631 (60)	2224 (157)	1927 (237)
AP5	624 (82)	617 (92)	1723 (135)	1707 (130)
AP group	**610 (12)**	**597 (31)**	**1965 (216)**	**1890 (150)**
MW1	758 (34)	791 (59)	2112 (179)	1960 (235)
MW2	703 (49)	664 (54)	1743 (141)	1772 (123)
MW3	748 (20)	643 (81)	1630 (253)	1622 (222)
MW4	729 (49)	696 (48)	1677 (190)	1695 (109)
MW5	807 (58)	751 (119)	1733 (193)	1658 (76)
MW group	**749 (39)**	**709 (62)**	**1779 (192)**	**1941 (134)**

Table 4.5 Individual and group averages (in Hz) for F_1 and F_2 values for pre-oral /æ/. Standard deviations are shown in parenthesis

Speaker	F_1		F_2	
	Midpoint	Offset	Midpoint	Offset
AA1	798 (79)	716 (143)	1891 (129)	1893 (177)
AA2	749 (133)	686 (126)	2114 (177)	2096 (164)
AA3	649 (95)	510 (113)	2051 (179)	1989 (221)
AA4	656 (80)	621 (57)	1904 (178)	2091 (233)
AA5	674 (82)	644 (78)	2095 (104)	2071 (164)
AA group	**682 (46)**	**635 (79)**	**2011 (106)**	**2028 (87)**
AP1	676 (96)	606 (61)	1885 (145)	1822 (143)
AP2	740 (113)	653 (103)	2763 (167)	2064 (261)
AP3	733 (86)	722 (77)	2084 (144)	2037 (153)
AP4	695 (49)	689 (64)	2093 (153)	2154 (153)
AP5	715 (57)	715 (58)	1955 (223)	1911 (223)
AP group	**712 (27)**	**677 (48)**	**2156 (351)**	**1998 (131)**
MW1	616 (46)	602 (51)	2374 (123)	2245 (354)
MW2	504 (141)	574 (146)	2093 (270)	1853 (335)
MW3	601 (52)	588 (61)	2213 (125)	2085 (112)
MW4	411 (123)	478 (149)	1955 (273)	1779 (244)
MW5	604 (47)	574 (49)	2127 (218)	1944 (127)
MW group	**547 (88)**	**563 (49)**	**2152 (155)**	**1981 (186)**

individual and group F_1 and F_2 averages. Recall from above that each average per speaker is based on 10–15 tokens.

Lowering of /ɛ/ and raising of /æ/ were selected primarily as features diagnostic of the Northern Cities Shift. However, raising of /æ/ in nasal environments specifically is a feature reported for contemporary AAE (Bailey and Thomas 1998) rather than a feature of NCS. Unsurprisingly, the five White Northerners follow the expected NCS pattern. All African American speakers also show a pattern of raising of /æ/ in nasal environments, but again, consistent with the findings of Labov (1994), Wolfram and Schilling-Estes (1998), and others, these speakers do not participate in other /ɛ/ and /æ/ patterns characteristic of the NCS. Nor do the Appalachian speakers show any sign of NCS participation with respect to these vowels. Their /ɛ/ and /æ/ patterns converge with those of the African Americans, but the

Table 4.6 Individual and group averages (in Hz) for F_1 and F_2 values for pre-nasal /æ/. Standard deviations are shown in parenthesis

Speaker	F_1		F_2	
	Midpoint	Offset	Midpoint	Offset
AA1	551 (116)	543 (125)	2087 (162)	2009 (334)
AA2	582 (83)	555 (75)	2091 (307)	2095 (354)
AA3	548 (115)	514 (121)	2132 (155)	2067 (207)
AA4	559 (83)	561 (61)	2277 (123)	2015 (193)
AA5	561 (101)	530 (119)	2115 (253)	1967 (236)
AA group	**560 (13)**	**541 (19)**	**2140 (79)**	**2031 (51)**
AP1	830 (144)	746 (62)	1906 (99)	1753 (50)
AP2	738 (42)	744 (47)	2013 (191)	1958 (124)
AP3	692 (30)	672 (26)	2324 (104)	2254 (149)
AP4	768 (6)	791 (14)	2133 (69)	2094 (437)
AP5	646 (75)	700 (49)	2134 (224)	1810 (150)
AP group	**735 (71)**	**731 (46)**	**2102 (156)**	**1974 (205)**
MW1	548 (150)	469 (163)	2239 (130)	2172 (75)
MW2	478 (257)	475 (250)	2042 (238)	2100 (153)
MW3	583 (49)	577 (29)	2299 (210)	1998 (166)
MW4	504 (118)	487 (147)	2191 (264)	1910 (231)
MW5	493 (71)	520 (85)	2276 (242)	1987 (153)
MW group	**521 (43)**	**506 (45)**	**2209 (102)**	**2033 (103)**

African Americans remain distinct from both Appalachian and White Northern groups with respect to their patterns of raising /æ/ in pre-nasal environments, thus indexing a linguistic boundary.

These data supplement the work on /ai/ reported above. Taken together, these pilot findings suggest that there are ongoing changes in the Detroit African American community which have the effect of distinguishing AAE speakers from White Northern speakers, but aligning them with speakers of some Southern varieties of English including the varieties spoken by Appalachian migrants to Detroit. The changes in question, which appear to have taken place over the last 40 years or so in the period since Wolfram carried out his work in Detroit, are (i) the fronting of the high and lower-high back vowels and (ii) the glide-weakening of /ai/ before voiceless obstruents.

5
Field Techniques and Acoustic Methods

This chapter describes the data collection and acoustic analysis, and the balance I have struck between sociolinguistic and phonetic types of methods. Whereas sociolinguists generally collect and analyze tokens taken from the spontaneous speech (or, sometimes, word-lists or reading passages) of many speakers, phoneticians typically collect more data from fewer speakers in a tightly controlled laboratory setting. Laboratory phoneticians often control for linguistic context and therefore do not use spontaneous speech. In this study, I followed the sociolinguistic practice of using spontaneous conversation collected in the field, but I obtained and analyzed as many tokens as possible across a range of phonetic contexts in an attempt to achieve a balanced corpus of tokens for the acoustic analysis. Section 5.1 provides an overview of sociolinguistic methods, including speaker selection, data collection, and data analysis. Section 5.2 describes the field methods used in this project, and Section 5.3 describes the methods for the acoustic analysis.

5.1 Study design

5.1.1 Speaker selection
The approach to speaker selection is a judgment sample which used a "snowball" technique. L. Milroy (1987a) describes the judgment sample as a procedure for which the researcher identifies particular types of speakers (based on demographic factors, for example) while planning a study and then attempts to locate and record such

speakers during the fieldwork phase of the study. Citing Wolfram (1969, 1974) and Milroy (1987b), she points out that relatively small judgment samples have yielded robust results for large-scale urban studies. Labov (1994, 2001), for example, used a judgment sample for his study of Philadelphia. Judgment samples have also been used successfully in studies of rural areas in North Carolina by Wolfram and his associates (e.g. Wolfram and Thomas 2002). Chambers (1995) describes random samples as impractical and comments that there seems to be consensus in the field that judgment samples are adequate for sociolinguistic studies.

Milroy and Gordon describe the snowball, or friend-of-a-friend, technique: "the researcher simply asks the subject to recommend other people who might be willing to participate in the study" (2003: 32). These researchers also note that an advantage of this technique is that it reduces the occurrence of the interviewer being rejected by potential participants. For this study, I asked participants (at the end of the interviews) if they could recommend other friends or family members who would be willing to help with the project. These leads were then followed up by my contacting these individuals, telling them about the project, and naming the other participant who recommended them. This technique was very successful in garnering interviews.

In addition to adopting and refining an approach to speaker selection, a researcher also has to determine how many speakers are needed. Although a larger number of speakers can lead to more robust results than a study with fewer speakers, there is a danger of doing a shallow analysis of many speakers. When looking at detailed phonetic data, more robust results may be obtained by analyzing many tokens over a range of phonetic contexts for a small number of speakers than by examining, for example, 5–10 tokens for a large number of speakers. Gordon (1997: 80) discusses the dilemma that sociophonetic researchers face as they design studies. He describes a "breadth–depth continuum"; at one end lie studies that involve a large number of participants or research sites but a small amount of data/tokens; at the other end lie studies that provide a thorough and detailed account of fewer participants or research sites. The approach I take, which is closer to the latter, is described in Section 5.1.3. The next section describes the fieldwork technique of participant observation and discusses some of the characteristics of ethnography.

5.1.2   Participant observation and ethnography

The friend-of-a-friend method used here for the data collection has been used successfully by Milroy (1987b) and Wolfram and his associates, among others. It is ethnographic in nature and involves participant observation. The benefit of this approach is that it allows the researcher to minimize the observer effect. A participant observer has some sort of tie to the relevant community, and a key principle of this approach to fieldwork, and interviewing in particular, is to allow the "interviewees" to initiate topics and control the direction of the conversation. I tried to obtain demographic information in the interviews that I conducted, but I did not use a pre-determined set of questions. I attempted to let the participants direct the conversation as much as possible. Participant observation is time-consuming because it requires the researcher to establish personal ties in the community which must be cultivated (Eckert 2000; Milroy and Gordon 2003). One must visit and participate in community get-togethers, build and maintain friendships, and engage in other time-intensive activities. Milroy and Gordon describe an important benefit of participant observation; it " . . . works well in small, well-delineated communities where suspicions about outsiders might inhibit other approaches to data collection" (2003: 70). For this study, the benefits of participant observation outweighed the limitations.

Studies which utilize participant observation often take an ethnographic approach (Eckert 2000, for example). One potential benefit of using an ethnographic approach is the possibility for the research to yield evidence of "local" categories, which eliminates the need to rely on preconceived and, often, controversial non-local categories such as social class (see Eckert 2000 for further discussion). As Eckert (2000: xiv) points out, the fundamental principle of ethnography is to "discover rather than impose." She highlights the need for researchers to discover and interpret relevant participant (i.e. local) categories, which requires consideration of practices which are meaningful to particular communities or groups. Eckert comments specifically on the main difference between approaches to fieldwork which utilize surveys with more ethnographic approaches: " . . . while survey fieldwork focuses on filling in a sample, ethnographic fieldwork focuses on finding out what is worth sampling" (2000: 69). One local category that emerged early in the fieldwork for this study was "Southern."

Many migrant participants, both White and Black as well as Southern-born (first generation) and Detroit-born (second/third generation), identified themselves as "Southern," and I observed a wide range of Southern cultural practices. As we shall see in Chapter 8, I argue that an enduring Southern regional identity for both the African American and the White migrant groups plays an important role in the vowel patterns analyzed in this study.

5.1.3 Data analysis

L. Milroy discusses an assumption that many sociolinguistic studies embody concerning variants of a variable, namely that they " . . . lie on a single phonetic continuum that corresponds to a social continuum" (1987a: 118). One problem with this type of analysis is that important information may be lost, especially for multidimensional and interacting factors. For example, acoustic properties such as formant frequencies are determined by overlapping articulatory movements. Second, many variationist studies do not attend to phonetic detail (but see a collection of papers edited by Foulkes and Docherty 1999 as well as Beckford 1999 and Thomas 1995, 2001), but instead use exclusively impressionistic approaches. Fine-grained phonetic detail is important to consider in investigations of phonological change because it can yield information about changes at stages between actuation and complete or nearly complete change, as suggested by J. Milroy (1992). More specifically, acoustic analysis can account for gradient variants that impressionistic coding may miss.

The process of gradual linguistic change can only be understood by examining frequencies of use of forms that vary across continual phonetic dimensions. This type of modeling thus requires gradient, not binary, observations. In the early and middle stages of sound change, phonetic variants of a variable may be in competition (Milroy 1992). For example, the data reported in Anderson (2001) show two competing phonetic forms for word final /d/ in Detroit AAE: [ʔ] (with no oral closure) and [ʔd] (with oral closure). These variants appear to be alternate realizations in Detroit AAE, and a fully glottal variant may be replacing the canonical supralaryngeal realization of /d/ in this dialect. In these cases, consideration of the phonetic details of the glottalization process is necessary in order to uncover the detailed information needed to trace a subtle shift from one stage of change to another. And it is these understudied stages that may provide new insight into the actuation of sound change and its early progress in establishing a new variant. Impressionistic reports can also be influenced by categorical perception (e.g. Repp 1982) and a failure to use the appropriate phonetic transcription. For example, it is not always possible to determine impressionistically whether a word-final voiceless stop such as /t/ is released or not (see further Foulkes and Docherty 1999). Such features are important to consider, for example, in discussions of complex phonological processes such as lenition. Instrumental phonetic research is crucial to testing the generalizations based on impressionistic studies of language variation.

It is especially important to take a gradient approach in the treatment of socially salient /ai/, one of the most socially meaningful vowels of American English (Wolfram and Schilling-Estes 1998), and glide-reduced variants are iconic markers of Southern and African American varieties. As Thomas (1995, 2001) observes, the duration of the glide varies considerably between fully diphthongal variants, nuclei with short offglides, and completely monophthongal variants. Categorizing tokens of /ai/ as strictly monophthongal or diphthongal may be misleading because it potentially eliminates important information about the duration and direction of the glide. It is for these reasons that I take a gradient approach for the analysis of the vowels in this study. The next section discusses approaches to data analysis in sociolinguistics.

5.1.4 Individual first versus community first

I take as a starting point the in-depth analysis of a small number of speakers, rather than a more superficial analysis (acoustically speaking) of many speakers. Examining individual speakers in detail will contribute to a growing movement toward what has been termed a "sociolinguistics of speakers" (Milroy 1992: 164–165; Johnstone 2000). As J. Milroy (1992) points out, the chief focus of Labovian sociolinguistics is not so much speakers but systems. Labov (2001: 33–34) argues against granting individual speakers a special place in sociolinguistic analysis:

> The behavior of the individual speaker cannot be understood until the sociolinguistic pattern of the community as a whole is delineated . . . The concept of the speech community and not

the idiolect is the primary object of linguistic investigation . . . The individual speaker can only be understood as . . . the intersection of the linguistic patterns of all the social groups and categories that define that individual. Linguistic analysis cannot recognize individual . . . phonologies . . . The individual does not exist as a linguistic object.

Taking a different view of the relevance of individual speakers to linguistic research, Johnstone (2000: 420) argues that the linguistics of language cannot achieve explanatory adequacy without a linguistics of individual speakers. She points out that " . . . variationist sociolinguistics . . . (typically treats) . . . individuals (as) operational-ized . . . bundles of demographic facts, and an individual's linguistic behavior is . . . seen as determined by these facts . . . Correlation is treated as if it were causation. . . . " (414).

Recognizing the relevance of "individual phonologies" does not negate the importance of speech communities or preclude the vari-ationist enterprise. Johnstone (2000) argues that traditional Labovian sociolinguistic analysis of systems rather than speakers can only be enriched by greater understanding of the linguistic behavior of indi-viduals, especially if individuals use language variation as a resource for expressing identity and if some changes originate in such expres-sion. In other words,

Thinking about variation from the individual outward rather than from the social inward means thinking about how individuals create unique voices by selecting and combining the linguistic resources available to them (417).

One can view speakers as repositories of social facts and "hosts to particular phonological systems" (as characterized in Watt 1998), or as agents who actively create and recreate identities and organize their own social behavior (Eckert 2000, Johnstone 2000), continu-ally making sociolinguistic choices during speech production. While acknowledging the vital importance of large-scale studies of speech communities, the methodology in this study aims to supple-ment these more traditional approaches by employing a bottom-up approach that carefully describes particular cases, namely the phonetic behavior of specific individuals. The next section describes the field methods.

5.2 Field methodology

5.2.1 Participants

The pilot study discussed in Chapter 4 revealed the African American and Appalachian White Southern migrant communities to be self-defined groups that maintain clear boundaries from Midwestern Whites. Building on these results, this study examines targeted portions of the vowel systems of 12 first- and second-/third-generation Appalachian White and African American migrant women.

As discussed in Section 5.1.1, selection of participants combined the friend-of-a-friend method and the judgment sample. Participants were categorized as first generation if they moved to the Detroit area from the South after the age of 18. Second-/third-generation speakers were either born and raised in Michigan or moved with their parents when they were less than five years old. Second- and third-generation migrants are not differentiated because what is crucial is that speakers in both groups attended school in Michigan and were exposed to Midwestern speech patterns in school and during local activities. In contrast, first-generation speakers moved from the South to relocate to the Detroit area after their dialect patterns were presumably already established. Although adults can and sometimes do adopt some phonetic features of a second dialect after migration (e.g. Munro *et al.* 1999), first-generation speakers presumably had well-established phonetic and phonological norms at the time of their move to Detroit (Chambers 1992).

Demographic information for participants is given in Table 5.1. The "core" sample consists of five second-/third-generation women from each of the Appalachian White and African American groups. For purposes of comparison, the core sample is supplemented by data gathered from one first-generation speaker from the African American group and one from the Appalachian White group, as well as one Midwestern White woman. The central comparison in this study is between the African American and Appalachian White Southern migrant groups. The role of the Midwestern White participant is

Table 5.1   Speaker sample for the acoustic study

Speaker	Ethnicity	Year of birth	Generation	Group (G), Individual (I), or Dyad (D)	Fieldworker
1	AA	1927	1	D	BA, TD
2	AA	1936	2	I	BA, SF
3	AA	1971	3	D	BA
4	AA	1974	3	D	BA
5	AA	1974	3	G	BA
6	AA	1967	3	I	BA
African American participants *N* = 6					
7	AP	1931	1	I	BA
8	AP	1960	2	I	SF
9	AP	1951	2	D	BA
10	AP	1949	2	I	BA, MA
11	AP	1936	2	I	BA
12	AP	1965	3	D	BA
Appalachian White participants *N* = 6					
13	MW WHITE	1967	N/A	G	SF
Midwestern White participants *N* = 1					
Total participants *N* = 13					

AA = African American; AP = Appalachian White; MW White = Midwestern White; BA = Myself; MA = White Male fieldworker; SF = White Female fieldworker; TD = African American female fieldworker.

simply to establish a basis of comparison for the analysis of individual speakers; the Hillenbrand *et al.* (1995) study is also used this way (see Section 5.4). The ambient Midwestern White dialect is quite different (see further Eckert 1988, 1989, 1991, 1996, 2000, 2001) from the AAE and Appalachian White dialects, which are similar in important respects (see further Edwards 1997; Hartigan 1999). African American participants are Detroit residents. With the exception of Speaker 8, the Appalachian White participants live in the inner suburbs. Speaker 13, a Midwestern White, also lives in an inner suburb. The fieldwork sites were discussed in Chapter 3.

5.2.2 Fieldwork and data collection

The fieldwork methods and data collection procedures used in the pilot study were also used for the main study (see Section 4.1). I carried out the fieldwork in the African American and Appalachian communities, with two exceptions (see Table 5.1). Susan Frekko, a graduate student in anthropology, conducted the fieldwork in the Midwestern White community and interviewed one of the Appalachian White participants. Tamika Davis, an African American Detroit resident, participated in an interview I conducted with one of the African American participants. Linguistics graduate student Mark Arehart also participated in an interview with one of the Appalachian White participants.

I began fieldwork in a Detroit West Side African American community in the winter of 1999. I developed close ties with several key participants and participated in a wide range of activities in the community, such as family get-togethers, holidays, parties, and meals. I engaged in relatively unstructured ethnographic observation to obtain a general sense of relevant attitudes, norms, and communicative conventions. One of the first African American participants introduced me to several of her friends and family that wanted to participate in the study. When I set up interviews, I told participants that I was interested in learning about the everyday lives of Detroit residents and wanted to record conversations in Motown at the turn of the century. The resultant conversations centered around the topics of everyday life, changes in Detroit, family history, and ties to the South. Fieldwork with African American participants was concluded in Fall 2001.

Fieldwork with the Appalachian participants began in the winter of 2001 and concluded in the spring of 2002. My initial contacts with this community were made through letters to the editors of newspapers in the Smoky Mountains of North Carolina, where I grew up. I asked readers to contact me or members of my family (who still reside in the Smokies) if they had relatives in the Detroit area. This contact information easily led to interviews with the Appalachian participants, a process that was doubtless facilitated by my Appalachian (specifically Smoky Mountain) origins. Like the African American participants, I told these participants that I was interested in the everyday lives of Southern migrants in Detroit and wanted to record conversations in Motown at the beginning of a new century. All the Appalachian participants self identified as being from the Smoky Mountains of Western North Carolina (even if it was in fact their parents or grandparents who migrated) except for one participant (8), whose parents migrated from rural West Virginia, interviewed by Susan Frekko. The topics in the Frekko interview were similar to the topics that came up in the interviews that I conducted (see below).

Table 5.1 shows that third parties were present in some of the interviews. The husbands of Speakers 1 and 3, who are also of Southern origin, participated in the interviews with their wives. Speaker 5 was interviewed along with two of her friends, who were also the descendants of Southern migrants. Speaker 9's mother, a Southern migrant, participated in her interview. Speaker 12's husband, a Midwesterner, participated in her interview; this is the only interview with a Southern migrant that also included a Midwesterner. However, data for Speaker 12 did not deviate in any significant way from that of the other participants.

As noted above, although I tried to obtain demographic information in the interviews that I conducted, I did not use a pre-determined set of questions. I started interviews by asking participants to give their years of birth. I then asked when their families moved up from the South. At this point in the interview, participants were encouraged to direct the conversation as much as possible. All the Southern migrant participants, both White and African American, described their families' migration histories as well as the difficulties they encountered in Detroit. Each participant described culturally important activities such as extended visits down South, family reunions, differences and similarities between the South and Detroit, and preparation and enjoyment of Southern food. In short, each of the participants expressed cultural orientations to and a regional affiliation with the South, even if she was Detroit-born; these cultural orientations will be described in Chapter 7.

Each participant described her work during the interview. Speakers 1, 8, and 9 are housewives. Speaker 2 is a retired gerontologist. Speakers 4 and 5 are college students, and Speaker 5 also works part-time in an automobile factory. Speaker 6 is an ad representative at a Christian radio station. Speakers 7 and 10 are retired factory workers. Speaker 9 is a factory worker who was laid off at the time of the interview. Speaker 13, the Midwestern White participant, is a secretary. All the speakers except for the college students own their homes. In addition to the college students, Speaker 2 has an undergraduate degree from Wayne State University. However, her vowel patterns are very similar to those of the other older African American speaker (Speaker 1).

It is important to note that none of the speakers' vowel data departed from group norms in any significant way. For the analysis of /u/ and /ʊ/, both Black and White Southern migrant participants show strikingly similar patterns of fronting. Even age was not statistically significant for fronting (see further Chapter 6).

For /ai/, the two older African American speakers show the traditional pattern for /ai/ described in the literature as typical of African American systems. The younger African American speakers also showed striking similarities for patterning of /ai/. They, along with the Appalachian White speakers, show glide-weakening in the progressive pre-voiceless context (see further Chapter 7). In other words, the data do not suggest that any of the speakers deviate from group norms for the variables in this study. To the contrary, there is relative uniformity across the data set, even across ethnic lines, for these Southern migrant participants.

5.2.3 Recording procedures

Interviews were audio-recorded using a Sony portable minidisk recorder (model MZ-R30) and a Sony microphone (model ECM-MS957). Care was taken in all the interviews to ensure the best acoustic environment possible under the circumstances; for example, fans were shut off, kitchens avoided, and carpeted rooms used if available.

5.3 Acoustic analysis

The recordings were digitized at a sampling rate of 22 kHz and lowpass filtered at 11 kHz. As in the pilot study, the Praat program was used for the acoustic analysis. I extracted a subset of the stressed vowel tokens from 60 minutes of casual conversation for each participant. Sections 5.3.1 and 5.3.2 describe the two types of acoustic measures used in this study. Vowels before consonants which triggered substantial coarticulatory effects, specifically nasals, /l/ and /ɹ/, were excluded in order to reduce the size of the data set and simplify the analysis.

5.3.1 Temporal locations and measures

Measurements were taken at two temporal locations in each vowel centered at vowel midpoint and 25 ms from the vowel offset. Figure 5.1 shows an example of manual placement of markers for vowel onset, midpoint, and offset. Vowel onset and offset were based on waveform displays, with vowel onset identified as the first recognizable quasiperiodic pitch pulse of the vowel and offset as the last recognizable quasiperiodic pitch pulse of the vowel (at the zero crossings).

5.3.2 Spectral measures

In addition to vowel duration measures, frequency measures for the first, second, and third formants (F_1, F_2, F_3) were taken for each vowel. Formant measurements were taken from FFT spectra, using a 0.025-s Gaussian window for analysis. I chose FFT analysis with a relatively wide window size because it provided a clear "snapshot" (Johnson 2003) of the formant frequencies. Measurements were taken by positioning cursors at the center of the highest amplitude harmonic excited by a given formant. Figure 5.2 shows an FFT spectrum of /ɪ/ midpoint with the first three formants marked by arrows.

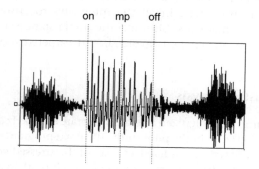

Figure 5.1 Locations of vowel onset (on), midpoint (mp) and offset (off) in the word "teach" produced by Speaker 6

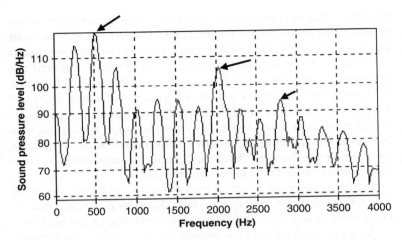

Figure 5.2 FFT spectrum centered at the midpoint of the vowel in [Kʰɪds] "kids" (Speaker 6). Locations of the first three formants, which are measured in Hz, are marked with arrows

5.4 Spectral comparisons

This study analyzes /i ɪ u ʊ o ɑ ai/ for the speakers listed in Table 5.1. I am primarily interested not in absolute formant frequencies, but rather in relative formant values of (potentially) spectrally similar vowels, in view of possible fronting of /u/ and /ʊ/ and glide-weakening of /ai/. Table 5.2 gives the average number of tokens per speaker and the average number of tokens per vowel, per phonetic environment, per speaker. The large standard deviations can be attributed to a number of factors. Tokens were taken for each speaker

Table 5.2 Total number of tokens per vowel pair

Tokens of ai/ɑ	1729
Tokens of I/ʊ	1569
Tokens of i/u	1664
Tokens of o	897
Total	5859

from one hour of conversation. However, some speakers were interviewed alone while others were interviewed as part of a dyad or small group (see Section 5.3). Therefore some speakers yielded more tokens than others. There was also variation in the number of tokens per phonetic environment, which was due to the unpredictable nature of spontaneous conversation. Even when topics of conversation are similar, there are often differences for the occurrences of particular lexical items and token types. For example, some vowels (such as /ʊ/) occur less commonly than other vowels (such as /ɪ/). While one speaker may use the word "book" and "took" five times each, another may produce much fewer tokens of pre-velar /ʊ/.

Measurements were taken at two temporal locations, described above, for each of the 5859 vowel tokens. No more than five instances per speaker of any given lexical item were included in the analysis.

The analysis of /u/ and /ʊ/ focuses on the F_2 distances between /u/ and /ʊ/ and /i/ and /ɪ/, respectively. All four vowels are typically classified in the high region: /u/ and /i/ as high and /ʊ/ and /ɪ/ as lower-high. Members of the vowel pairs /u/–/i/ and /ʊ/–/ɪ/ differ little in F_1, which correlates primarily with vowel height. However, members of these pairs differ in F_2. Front-back tongue body position affects F_2, as does lip rounding (particularly for back vowels) (Stevens 1998: 273). Vowels that are more front and less rounded have relatively high F_2 frequencies and small F_2–F_3 separation. Vowels that are rounded and back have relatively low F_2 frequencies and a large F_2–F_3 separation.

Fronting of /u/ and /ʊ/ was quantified for each speaker by calculating the difference between the average F_2 values of /u/ and /ʊ/ and their front counterparts /i/ and /ɪ/ (see further Anderson 2003). Using the average distance between front and back counterparts, rather than the absolute F_2 measure of the back vowels, allows for cross-speaker comparisons. If a hypothetical Speaker A has a significantly smaller F_2 distance between /i/ and /u/ than Speaker B, then Speaker A can be said to have a more fronted /u/. Note that this measure does not categorize Speaker A's /u/ as "front" and Speaker B's as "back." It is strictly a relative measure that allows one to describe the vowels as more or less front. The comparison assumes that /i/ and /ɪ/ are both stable front vowels. Otherwise, the shorter distance could indicate backing of /i/ or a combination of /i/ backing and /u/ fronting. Since all speakers are women, it is assumed that their overall F_1/F_2 spaces

Table 5.3 Tokens of /ʊ/ and /ɪ/ per speaker and per following environment

Speaker	/ʊ/ alv	/ʊ/ velar	/ɪ/ alv	/ɪ/ velar	Total
1	8	11	58	18	95
2	25	6	69	30	130
3	17	10	72	23	122
4	25	5	88	35	153
5	28	9	93	20	150
6	30	13	61	27	131
7	27	13	74	25	139
8	21	6	70	28	125
9	30	12	84	32	158
10	25	13	99	31	168
11	17	10	58	14	99
12	15	10	44	30	99
	268	118	870	313	1569

alv = pre-alveolar; velar = pre-velar.

are comparably sized. However, it is important to note that the use of distance measures renders normalization, which is highly controversial (Johnson 1989), unnecessary.

For /u/, distances were calculated separately for three environments (pre-labial, pre-alveolar, and word-final) at midpoint and offset. The pre-velar environment was not examined due to an insufficient number of tokens. Each speaker therefore has six different /u/ fronting scores (three contexts and two temporal locations). For /ʊ/, there were only two environments, pre-alveolar and pre-velar, resulting in four /ʊ/ fronting scores (two contexts and two temporal locations). Pre-labial /ʊ/ was not examined due to too few tokens, and word-final /ʊ/ is phonotactically disallowed in English. Table 5.3 gives the breakdown of tokens of /ʊ/and/ɪ/ by speaker and following environment, and Table 5.4 gives these same figures for /u/ and /i/.

Group comparisons of pre-alveolar tokens of /u/ and /ʊ/produced by the African American and Appalachian White groups are also made with those reported for a reference group of 48 Midwestern White Kalamazoo women in the Hillenbrand *et al.* (1995) study. This group is included to provide a benchmark rather than to serve as a third group;

Table 5.4   Tokens of /u/ and /i/ per speaker and per following environment

Speaker	/u/ alv	/u/ wb	/u/ lab	/i/ alv	/i/ wb	/i/ lab	Total
1	8	15	4	15	31	20	93
2	14	29	8	60	20	30	161
3	20	16	6	22	37	12	113
4	30	26	11	39	22	44	172
5	24	35	11	54	34	43	201
6	13	38	9	61	34	20	175
7	19	28	7	28	21	16	119
8	21	26	11	36	27	13	134
9	19	30	10	27	20	19	125
10	22	28	13	22	31	29	145
11	19	23	9	30	24	16	121
12	21	22	8	23	20	11	105
	230	316	107	417	321	273	1664

alv = alveolar; wb = pre-pausal or pre-word boundary; lab = pre – labial.

as noted in Section 5.2.1, the central comparisons in this study are between Appalachian White and African American Southern migrant participants because of the linguistic similarities between these two groups that were revealed in the pilot study (see Chapter 4). Data from Speaker 13 (the Detroit White) is used to examine contrasting /ai/ realizations while the Hillenbrand *et al.* participants are used to examine contrasting patterns of high and lower-high back vowel fronting. Only pre-alveolar tokens were amenable to comparisons between these two Southern migrant groups and the Kalamazoo women because Hillenbrand *et al.* limited their measurements to this environment (*h_d*) at midpoint. A limitation of this comparison is that data for the Southern migrants comes from spontaneous conversation while data from the Hillenbrand *et al.*'s study is taken from word lists. In addition, Hillenbrand *et al.* screened participants by recording a 5–7-minute conversation with one of the experimenters which was later reviewed. Participants who showed " . . . any systematic departure from general American English" were not included in the subsequent acoustic study. Thus, an important difference between my study and the Hillenbrand *et al.*'s study is that I am interested in "vernacular" rather than "Standard" (or mainstream) vowel productions. However, as noted above, the most important comparisons for the purposes of this study are between the African American

Table 5.5 Tokens of /ai/ and /ɑ/ according to speaker and following environment

Speaker	/ai/ vd	/ai/ vless	/ɑ/ vd	/ɑ/ vless	Total
1	31	39	18	9	108
2	53	68	36	42	229
3	24	40	17	7	96
4	33	56	46	21	166
5	33	38	49	36	176
6	45	30	26	17	132
7	28	29	22	23	112
8	22	23	36	21	116
9	23	33	24	15	121
10	54	23	29	25	159
11	17	21	20	21	98
12	21	19	20	18	98
13	43	22	26	12	118
	427	441	369	267	1729

vd = pre-voiced; vless = pre-voiceless; wb = pre-pausal or pre-word boundary.

and Appalachian White Southern migrant speakers. The Hillenbrand *et al.* speakers are simply included as a non-fronting reference group.

Participants in the Hillenbrand *et al.* study read lists containing 12 vowels, including /u/, /i/, /ʊ/, /ɪ/, and /o/, and one token of each vowel from each participant was analyzed in terms of F_1, F_2, and F_3 measures taken at vowel midpoint. Despite the differences in the study design for this study and the study design used in Hillenbrand *et al.*, the comparison is useful for showing the difference between fronted and backed variants of /u/ and /ʊ/. Chapter 6 shows that while the Southern migrants show fronted variants of these back vowels, the Hillenbrand *et al.* speakers do not.

The analysis of /ai/ quantifies diphthongization by comparing F_1 and F_2 movement in /ai/, which exhibits varying degrees of diphthongization, with F_1 and F_2 movement in /ɑ/, which is used as a reference because it is expected to show little, if any, diphthongization. The differences between midpoint and measurements taken 25 ms before the end of the offset in F_1 and F_2 were calculated for /ɑ/ and /ai/. The nature of the patterning in terms of voicing context is examined because previous studies have described strong contextual effects for monophthongization and glide-weakening of /ai/ based on the voicing of the following consonant (see Section 2.2 for a summary; see also Thomas 2001). Data from the participants in the Hillenbrand *et al.* (1995) study were not included in the group comparisons, as they were for the analysis of /u/ and /ʊ/, because /ai/ was not analyzed in that study. However, data from Speaker 13, a Detroit Midwestern White woman, is included in the discussion of individual speakers. Table 5.5 gives the breakdown of /ai/ and /ɑ/according to speaker and following environment.

6
The High and Lower-High Back Vowels

This chapter reports the acoustic findings for /u/ and /ʊ/, which are examined in relation to the front vowels, /i/ and /ɪ/. Fronting is quantified by examining /u/∼/i/ and /ʊ/∼/ɪ/ F_2 distances (see further Section 5.4). Section 6.1 describes the fronting patterns of /u/ and /ʊ/ of the African American (AA) and Appalachian White (AP) groups with attention to contextual effects. Section 6.2 analyzes the effects of consonantal context, considering the interactions of context, Vowel quality, vowel duration, and their effects on fronting. Section 6.3 discusses the combined effects of rounding and backing. Section 6.4 discusses Nguyen's (2006) real-time analysis of /ʊ/ by social status for Detroit AAs. Section 6.5 presents the results of Nguyen and Anderson's (2006) comparisons of /u/ fronting among AA and Midwestern White speakers in the Detroit area. The chapter concludes with a summary and emphasizes the importance of considering the role of phonetic context when examining vowel changes in American English.

Systematic analysis of context reveals patterns that would not otherwise be evident. Specifically, analysis of contexts which should (and should not) trigger fronting based on coarticulatory effects from following consonantal contexts reveals a pattern which demonstrates the need to consider the role of contextual conditioning in vowel changes. For /u/∼/i/ and /ʊ/∼/ɪ/ F_2 distances, both the AA and AP Southern migrant groups show small distance measures (i.e. more fronting) for pre-alveolar variants throughout the vowel (i.e. at both vowel midpoint and offset). Another consistent pattern was that pre-labial /u/ was consistently more back (larger /u/∼/i/ F_2 distances) for both groups. The only significant difference by ethnicity for the F_2

distance scores between the phonologically front and phonologically back vowels is that the AP speakers show a more back pre-velar /ʊ/ than the AA speakers.

Section 6.1 describes the patterns of fronting for the AA and AP Southern migrant groups by ethnicity, vowel, and following phonetic context at midpoint and offset.

6.1   Analysis of /u/~/i/ and /ʊ/~/ɪ/ distances at midpoint and offset

This section (1) provides a quantitative account of /u/ and /ʊ/ fronting, (2) determines to what extent, if any, the AA and AP speakers have similar patterns of fronting, and (3) determines the nature of the vowel patterning in terms of following consonantal context. The patterning of /u/ and /ʊ/ for the Southern migrant speakers is also compared to a reference group of speakers whose formant frequency values are reported by Hillenbrand *et al.* (1995) (see Section 5.4) Hillebrand *et al.*'s speakers have backed variants and thus provide a benchmark for fronting. The following section describes the data and methods. Section 6.1.2 provides a descriptive overview of the patterns by ethnicity, vowel, and context, and Section 6.1.3 gives a statistical analysis of these patterns.

6.1.1   Methods for the statistical analysis

The dataset for this portion of the study was described in Section 5.3 and a token list provided in Tables 5.5 and 5.6. The spectral comparisons discussed in this chapter are described in Section 5.4. F_2 distance measures between front and back counterparts allow the analyst to quantify fronting. A back vowel can only be judged as "fronted" when it is examined in relation to its phonologically front counterpart. In addition, analyzing F_2 values alone (without reference to their front counterparts) is problematic because of the normalization problem; formant values vary across individual speakers due to variations in vocal tract size. A comparison of the relationship between two elements within an individual speaker's system renders normalization unnecessary (see Section 5.4 and Anderson 2003).

Fronting of /u/ and /ʊ/ was quantified for each speaker by calculating the difference between the average F_2 values of /u/ and /ʊ/

and their front counterparts /i/ and /ɪ/. For /u/~/i/, distances were calculated separately for three environments (pre-labial, pre-alveolar, and word-final) at midpoint and offset. Each speaker therefore has six different /u/ fronting scores (three contexts and two temporal locations). For /ʊ/, there were only two environments, pre-alveolar and pre-velar, resulting in four /ʊ/ fronting scores (two contexts and two temporal locations). A high value for an F_2 distance is diagnostic of a backed variant while a low value is diagnostic of a fronted variant.

Testing for main effects and interactions of ethnicity and environment was conducted using General Linear Model (GLM) analysis of variance (using the SPSS statistical analysis program, version 11.0) for each of the four F_2 distance values (/u/~/i/ and /ʊ/~/ɪ/ at midpoint and offset). Age was not included in the main analysis of fronting of /u/ and /ʊ/ because several tests showed that it was not a significant factor and could therefore be omitted. The first test of age was to separate the F_2 values of the two oldest speakers in each group from the four youngest. I conducted a GLM analysis of variance at midpoint and offset for F_2 distances using the factors of age, ethnicity, and environment. The age factor had no significant main effect and did not participate in any significant interactions for midpoint or offset F_2 distances of either vowel pair.

The second method of testing age was a three-way classification of the speakers according to whether they are first-, second-, or third-generation migrants. The results of the analysis using this alternative classification were the same, with no significant main effect on F_2 distances for generation and no significant interactions. With 12 total speakers, it is best not to multiply the cross-classifications unnecessarily, and these tests show that age can be safely omitted. F_2 distance values are therefore separated into groups on the basis of ethnicity only.

6.1.2 Descriptive overview of fronting patterns

First, I compare data from the AA and AP speakers with those of the reference group of 48 female speakers from Hillenbrand *et al.* (1995) (see Section 5.4). Then I compare in more detail the AA and AP groups by vowel (/u/~/i/ and /ʊ/~/ɪ/) and context at both midpoint and offset.

6.1.2.1   African American, Appalachian, and Midwestern White groups

Figure 6.1 shows F_1 and F_2 midpoint values in the pre-alveolar context for the three groups of speakers. Only pre-alveolar tokens are included in this plot because Hillenbrand *et al.* limited their measurements to this environment (*h_d*) at midpoint. The lines in Figure 6.1 connect front and back counterparts for each group of speakers and the numbers are F_2 differences between them. /o/ provides a common reference area for the back of the vowel spaces for all of the groups. The figure shows that pre-alveolar /u/ midpoint is fronted for all the Detroit Southern migrant speakers regardless of ethnicity. In contrast, Hillenbrand *et al.* found that the 48 women in their study had an average /i/ F_2 midpoint value of 2761 Hz and /u/ value of 1105 Hz (standard deviation was not reported), which is a distance of 1656 Hz, several times greater than the 480 Hz pre-alveolar midpoint distance

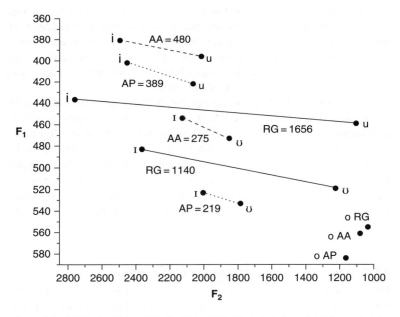

Figure 6.1   Midpoint F_1 and F_2 (in Hz) of /i/, /ɪ/, /u/, /ʊ/, and /o/ (pre-alveolar context) in Hz for the AA and AP speakers in this study and the reference group (RG) of 48 women from Hillenbrand *et al.* (1995). The lines connect front and back vowel counterparts and the numbers are distance in F_2

found here among the Detroit AA speakers and the 389 Hz for the AP speakers. The Detroit speakers also show a different pattern than the Hillenbrand *et al.* speakers for pre-alveolar /ʊ/. The female speakers in Hillenbrand *et al.*'s study (1995) have a midpoint distance of 1140 Hz, while the Detroit AA speakers show a distance of only 275 Hz and the Detroit AP speakers show a distance of 219 Hz. High F_2 values for /ʊ/ and /u/ and small F_2 distances for /ʊ/~/ɪ/ and /u/~/i/ indicate fronted variants for the AA and AP groups relative to the vowel productions of the speakers in Hillenbrand *et al.*'s study.

6.1.2.2   African American and Appalachian speakers

Fronting of /u/ and /ʊ/ is sensitive to the following phonetic environment for both Southern migrant groups. Figure 6.2 shows midpoint

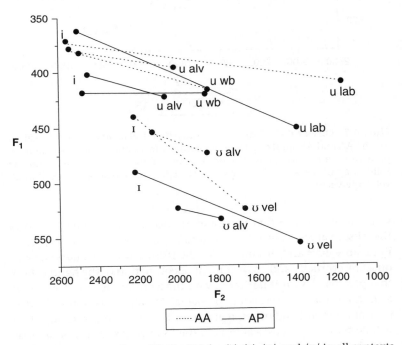

Figure 6.2   Midpoint F_1 and F_2 (in Hz) for /i/, /ɪ/, /u/, and /ʊ/ in all contexts measured for the AA and AP speakers. The lines connect front and back vowel counterparts in each environment. The dotted line represents AA speakers and the solid line, AP speakers alv = pre-alveolar, lab = pre-labial, wb = word-final, vel = pre-velar.

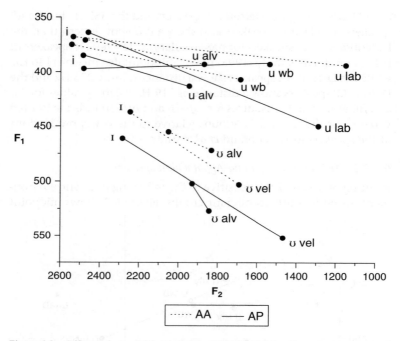

Figure 6.3   Offset values of /i/, /ɪ/, /u/, and /ʊ/ (in Hz) in all contexts measured for the AA and AP speakers. The lines connect front and back vowel counterparts in each environment. The dotted line represents AA speakers and the solid line, AP speakers. alv = pre-alveolar, lab = pre-labial, wb = word-final, vel = pre-velar

values in all contexts for the AA and AP speakers, and Figure 6.3 shows the offset values. Tables 6.1 (/u/ and /i/) and 6.2 (/ʊ/ and /ɪ/) show F_2 mean values and distance from the front vowels at midpoint and offset by ethnicity and environment. Examination of the figures show that pre-alveolar /u/ is farther toward the front of the vowel envelope at midpoint and offset, while pre-labial /u/ was consistently further back at midpoint and offset, regardless of ethnicity (observations that will be subject to statistical tests in the following section). As already seen in Figure 6.1, the fronting of pre-alveolar /u/ reported here for the speakers of Southern origin is not found for the reference group of female speakers in the Hillenbrand *et al.* (1995) study; those speakers show a much larger F_2 distance measure between pre-alveolar /u/ and

Table 6.1 F$_2$ of /i/ and /u/ and F$_2$ /i/~/u/ distance at midpoint and offset (in Hz) by ethnicity and following environment (N = number of speakers)

Environment	Ethnicity		Midpoint distance	Offset distance	/i/ midpoint	/u/ midpoint	/i/ offset	/u/ offset
Word-final	AA	Mean	700	859	2547	1846	2545	1686
		Stdev	357	380	204	317	188	366
		N	6	6	6	6	6	6
	AP	Mean	620	945	2479	1859	2484	1539
		Stdev	145	314	182	212	140	238
		N	6	6	6	6	6	6
Labial	AA	Mean	1374	1388	2543	1169	2539	1152
		Stdev	342	285	223	201	173	166
		N	6	6	6	6	6	6

Table 6.1 (Continued)

Environment	Ethnicity	Midpoint distance	Offset distance	/i/ midpoint	/u/ midpoint	/i/ offset	/u/ offset
	AP						
	Mean	1107	1172	2504	1397	2462	1290
	Stdev	377	358	201	317	169	275
	N	6	6	6	6	6	6
Alveolar	AA						
	Mean	480	597	2496	2016	2468	1871
	Stdev	200	238	131	216	136	282
	N	6	6	6	6	6	6
	AP						
	Mean	389	540	2453	2064	2487	1948
	Stdev	324	231	181	184	178	185
	N	6	6	6	6	6	6

Table 6.2 F$_2$ of /ɪ/ and /ʊ/ and F$_2$ /ɪ/~/ʊ/ distance at midpoint and offset (in Hz) by ethnicity and following environment (N = number of speakers)

Environment	Ethnicity	Midpoint distance	Offset distance	/ɪ/ midpoint	/ʊ/ midpoint	/ɪ/ offset	/ʊ/ offset
Alveolar	AA						
	Mean	275	219	2127	1852	2052	1833
	Stdev	175	106	186	121	177	113
	N	6	6	6	6	6	6
	AP						
	Mean	219	87	2004	1785	1931	1844
	Stdev	157	199	171	159	225	141
	N	6	6	6	6	6	6
Velar	AA						
	Mean	560	552	2222	1662	2245	1692
	Stdev	164	262	195	167	217	246
	N	6	6	6	6	6	6
	AP						
	Mean	832	817	2218	1386	2285	1468
	Stdev	225	220	96	234	109	223
	N	6	6	6	6	6	6

/i/. For /ʊ/, the pre-alveolar environment shows more fronting than pre-velar. Pre-velar tokens are further back in the vowel space than alveolars for both groups, but the AA speakers show more fronting for this environment than the Appalachian speakers. Below I describe these patterns in more detail.

For /u/ midpoint (Figure 6.2, Table 6.1), the pre-labial environment shows a greater F_2 distance between front and back pairs than either pre-alveolar or word-final pairs. The AA speakers show a mean F_2 distance of 1374 Hz at midpoint for pre-labial contexts and the AP speakers show a mean F_2 distance of 1107 Hz, compared to 480 Hz and 389 Hz in the pre-alveolar context. Word-final /u/ falls in the middle, with the AA speakers showing a mean F_2 distance of 700 Hz, and the AP speakers 620 Hz. The same pattern occurs at the offset (see Figure 6.3 and Table 6.1), with pre-labial showing the largest F_2 distance (1388 Hz for AA, 1172 Hz for AP), followed by word-final (859 Hz and 945 Hz), followed by pre-alveolar (597 Hz and 540 Hz). In the pre-labial environment, neither group shows much difference between midpoint and offset F_2 distances (a 14 Hz difference for the AA group and a 65 Hz difference for the AP group). In the pre-alveolar environment, both groups show a tendency to be less fronted at offset than at midpoint (the AA group by 117 Hz; the AP group by 151 Hz). The same pattern of movement toward the back of the vowel space occurs in the word-final environment: the AA group's difference is 139 Hz and the AP group's is 325 Hz.

The results for /ɪ/ and /ʊ/ at midpoint and offset by following phonetic environment and ethnicity are summarized in Table 6.2 and Figure 6.3. The F_2 distance between pre-alveolar /ɪ/ and /ʊ/ is 275 Hz at midpoint and 219 Hz at offset for the AA speakers and 219 Hz and 87 Hz for the AP speakers. Pre-velar F_2 distances are greater: 560 Hz (midpoint) and 552 Hz (offset) for the AA speakers and 832 Hz (midpoint) and 817 Hz (offset) for the AP speakers. Although both groups show less fronted variants for pre-velar than for pre-alveolar contexts, the AA group shows more pre-velar fronting than the AP group, a result to be discussed in greater detail in the following section. The AA and AP groups show a pattern in which the F_2 distance measure decreases from midpoint to offset (i.e. the offset is more fronted than the midpoint) due to the effect of the following consonantal context. The AA group shows that F_2 moves forward in the vowel envelope by 56 Hz, and the AP group shows F_2

movement toward the front of the vowel envelope of 132 Hz. The AA and AP speakers show differences for F_1 in that AP speakers have lower vowels (indicated by higher F_1 values) than the AA speakers, a pattern for which I lack an explanation at this point.

6.1.3 Statistical analysis of F_2 distances

As mentioned above, testing for main effects and interactions of ethnicity and environment was conducted using a GLM analysis of variance for /u/~/i/ F_2 distance and /ʊ/~/ɪ/ F_2 distance at the midpoint and offset, resulting in four tests. The results are shown in Tables 6.3–6.6. Whereas all four tests showed significant main effects for context, none showed a main effect for ethnicity. The significant main effects for context were as follows: for /u/~/i/ midpoint F_2 distance, $F(2,35) = 22.541$, $p < 0.001$; /u/~/i/ offset F_2 distance, $F(2,35) = 16.251$, $p < 0.001$; /ʊ/~/ɪ/ midpoint F_2 distance, $F(1,23) = 36.415$, $p < 0.001$; /ʊ/~/ɪ/ offset F_2 distance, $F(1,23) = 40.462$, $p < 0.001$. The non-significant main effects for ethnicity were as follows: /u/~/i/ midpoint F_2 distance, $F(1,35) = 2.084$, $p < 0.159$; /u/~/i/ offset F_2 distance, $F(1,35) = 0.371$, $p < 0.547$; /ʊ/~/ɪ/ midpoint F_2 distance, $F(1,23) = 2.114$, $p < 0.161$; /ʊ/~/ɪ/ offset F_2 distance, $F(1,23) = 0.628$, $p < 0.438$. For /u/ midpoint and offset, there is also no significant interaction between ethnicity and environment (midpoint $F(2,35) = 0.357$, $p < 0.702$; offset $F(2,35) = 0.729$, $p < 0.491$), indicating that ethnicity is not a significant factor in the fronting of /u/. For /ʊ/, there is a significant interaction both for midpoint ($F(1,23) = 4.882$, $p < 0.039$) and offset ($F(1,23) = 5.630$, $p < 0.028$), so to compare ethnicities it is necessary to look within environments. First, I will discuss main effects of environment for both vowels, then the interactions for /ʊ/.

For /u/, Tukey post-hoc analyses show that pre-labial F_2 distance for midpoint (Table 6.7) was significantly greater than both pre-alveolar, with a marginal mean difference of 806 Hz, and word-final F_2 distances, with a marginal mean distance of 580 Hz (midpoint: $p < 0.001$), while pre-alveolar and word-final contexts did not differ significantly from one another (marginal mean difference of 226 Hz). For the offset F_2 distances (Table 6.8), pre-labial was significantly greater than word-final, with a marginal mean difference of 378 Hz ($p < 0.014$), which was also significantly greater than pre-alveolar, with a marginal mean difference of 334 Hz ($p < 0.031$). For /ʊ/,

Table 6.3 ANOVA of main effects and interactions for /u/~/i/ midpoint F_2 distance

Dependent variable: midpoint distance

Source	Type III sum of squares	df	Mean square	F	Sig.
CONTEXT	4 146 857.056	2	2 073 428.528	22.541	0.000
ETH	191 698.028	1	191 698.028	2.084	0.159
CONTEXT * ETH	65 747.722	2	32 873.861	0.357	0.702
Error	2 759 525.500	30	91 984.183		
Total	28 974 285.0	36			
Corrected total	7 163 828.306	35			

Table 6.4 ANOVA of main effects and interactions for /u/~/i/ offset F_2 distance

Dependent variable: offset distance

Source	Type III sum of squares	df	Mean square	F	Sig.
CONTEXT	3 044 838.722	2	1 522 419.361	16.251	0.000
ETH	34 720.111	1	34 720.111	0.371	0.547
CONTEXT * ETH	136 621.722	2	68 310.861	0.729	0.491
Error	2 810 428.000	30	93 680.933		
Total	36 272 942.0	36			
Corrected total	6 026 608.556	35			

Table 6.5 ANOVA of main effects and interactions for /ʊ/~/ɪ/ midpoint F_2 distance

Dependent variable: midpoint distance

Source	Type III sum of squares	df	Mean square	F	Sig.
CONTEXT	1 207 362.042	1	1 207 362.042	36.415	0.000
ETH	70 092.042	1	70 092.042	2.114	0.161
CONTEXT * ETH	161 868.375	1	161 868.375	4.882	0.039
Error	663 117.167	20	33 155.858		
Total	7 435 105.000	24			
Corrected total	2 102 439.625	23			

Table 6.6   ANOVA of main effects and interactions for /ʊ/~/ɪ/ offset F_2 distance

Dependent variable: offset distance

Source	Type III sum of squares	df	Mean square	F	Sig.
CONTEXT	1 697 612.042	1	1697612.042	40.462	0.000
ETH	26 334.375	1	26334.375	0.628	0.438
CONTEXT * ETH	236 215.042	1	236215.042	5.630	0.028
Error	839 112.500	20	41955.625		
Total	7 003 525.000	24			
Corrected total	2 799 273.958	23			

Table 6.7   Tukey post-hoc analysis on the environment factor for /u/~/i/ midpoint F_2 distance

Dependent variable: midpoint distance
Tukey HSD

(I) context	(J) context	Mean difference (I − J)	Std. error	Sig.	95% Confidence interval	
					Lower bound	Upper bound
Word-final	Labial	−580*	124	0.000	−885	−275
	Alveolar	226	124	0.180	−80	531
Labial	Word-final	580*	124	0.000	275	885
	Alveolar	806*	124	0.000	501	1111
Alveolar	Word-final	−226	124	0.180	−531	80
	Labial	−806*	124	0.000	−1111	−501

Based on observed means.
* The mean difference is significant at the 0.05 level.

there were only two environments, pre-alveolar and pre-velar, so the Tukey post-hoc test is not applicable. As noted previously and seen in Table 6.2, the pre-velar F_2 distance was greater than pre-alveolar at both midpoint (by 285 Hz for the AA group and 613 Hz for the AP group) and offset (333 Hz for AA, 730 Hz for AP). In general then, for /u/, pre-alveolar and word-final tokens are more fronted (with the pre-alveolar environment showing a greater degree of fronting

Table 6.8 Tukey post-hoc analysis on the environment factor for /u/~/i/ offset F_2 distance

Dependent variable: midpoint distance
Tukey HSD

(I) context	(J) context	Mean difference (I − J)	Std. error	Sig.	95% Confidence interval	
					Lower bound	Upper bound
Word-final	Labial	−378*	125	0.014	−686	−70
	Alveolar	334*	125	0.031	26	642
Labial	Word-final	378*	125	0.014	70	686
	Alveolar	712*	125	0.000	404	1020
Alveolar	Word-final	−334*	125	0.031	−642	−26
	Labial	−712*	125	0.000	−1020	−404

Based on observed means.
* The mean difference is significant at the .05 level.

than word-final), and pre-labial is backed. For /ʊ/, pre-alveolar tokens show fronting while pre-velar tokens are more backed.

Comparison of ethnicities within environments for /ʊ/-/ɪ/ F_2 distance was analyzed using the estimated marginal means and 95% confidence intervals shown in Tables 6.9 and 6.10. For the midpoint in the pre-alveolar context, the AA group's F_2 distance was just 56 Hz greater than the AP group, and each mean is contained in the

Table 6.9 Estimated marginal means for /ʊ/~/ɪ/ F_2 distance at midpoint, by ethnicity and context

Dependent variable: midpoint distance

Ethnicity	Context	Mean	Std. error	95% Confidence interval	
				Lower bound	Upper bound
AA	Alveolar	275	74.337	120	430
	Velar	560	74.337	404	715
AP	Alveolar	219	74.337	64	374
	Velar	832	74.337	677	987

Table 6.10 Estimated marginal means for /ʊ/~/ɪ/ F_2 distance at offset, by ethnicity and context

Dependent variable: offset distance

Ethnicity	Context	Mean	Std. error	95% Confidence interval	
				Lower bound	Upper bound
AA	Alveolar	219	83.622	44	393
	Velar	552	83.622	378	727
AP	Alveolar	87	83.622	−88	261
	Velar	817	83.622	642	991

other group's confidence interval. In the pre-velar context, however, the AA group's /ʊ/~/ɪ/ F_2 distance was 272 Hz less than the AP group. Although each group's mean is beyond the other's confidence interval, the ends of the intervals overlap somewhat, with 715 Hz as the upper bound on the AA group's estimate and 677 Hz as the lower bound on the AP group's estimate. So, although the difference for the /ʊ/~/ɪ/ F_2 distance between the groups is greater within the pre-velar context, the difference is not great enough to be deemed significant in itself. For offset /ʊ/~/ɪ/ F_2 distance, in the pre-alveolar environment the AA group had a greater distance than the AP group by 132 Hz, and each mean is contained within the other group's confidence interval. In the pre-velar environment, however, the AA group had a smaller /ʊ/~/ɪ/ F_2 distance than the AP group by 265 Hz. The pattern is the same as at midpoint, with the AA's upper bound of 727 Hz overlapping with the AP's lower bound of 642 Hz. The overall interaction pattern is that the AA group has slightly greater /ʊ/~/ɪ/ F_2 distance values in the pre-alveolar context and the AP group has much larger F_2 distance values in the pre-velar context, even though the differences were not significant when considered individually.

6.1.4 Summary and significance of the F_2 distance results

Fronting of /u/ and /ʊ/ among the Detroit AA and AP southern migrant speakers is sensitive to the following phonetic environment. Pre-alveolar /u/ midpoint is farther toward the front of the vowel envelope than pre-labial /u/ for the AP and AA speakers regardless of ethnicity. The pre-alveolar /u/~/i/ and /ʊ/~/ɪ/ F_2 distance measures were compared to the values reported in Hillenbrand *et al.* (1995); the female speakers in that study show large values for the F_2 distances on the order of four times those found for the AA and AP women in this study. In other words, the AA and AP southern migrant groups show contextually conditioned patterns of fronting for the high back vowels, while the reference group from the Hillenbrand *et al.* study does not show patterns of fronting. Patterns of fronting with regard to context effects from the following consonant are examined in more detail in section 6.2.

6.2 Context effects of consonants on preceding vowels

This section discusses following consonantal effects on vowel quality and duration and their role in distinguishing between ethnicities. Context effects are the result of coarticulation. The acoustic effects of coarticulation are lawful and predictable, arising out of acoustic–articulatory relations. Given the lawful nature of patterns of coarticulation, different dialects would not be expected to show opposite directions of shifts based on context effects. However, as cross-linguistic work on coarticulation suggests (e.g. Beddor *et al.* 2002), different dialects may well show different degrees for the progression of contextually conditioned shifts. Analysis of context effects may yield important information about the progression of sound change across individual speakers as well as dialects. However, context effects are not always analyzed in socioacoustic work on American English vowel systems. Following phonetic environment has important effects on the patterning of the vowels for the speakers in this study. Context effects from the following consonant on the vowels /u/ and /ʊ/ are assessed at two temporal locations: vowel midpoint and 25 ms before the end of the offset.

There are good reasons for taking formant measurements at both the midpoint and offset portions of the vowel. Watt (1998) discusses the tendency in socioacoustic work on vowel systems to take measurements only at a "steady state" in an attempt to avoid heavily coarticulated onsets and offsets. However, the situation is not so straightforward as this. Watt (1998: 29–30) points out that perceptual research has shown that listeners make use of a range of information distributed throughout the duration of segment and especially for vowels at the heavily coarticulated boundary and transition zones between vowels and consonants (Ohala 1992). Childs (2005), Thomas (2001),

Bailey and Thomas (1998), and Wolfram and Thomas (2002) are exceptions in that offset as well as midpoint formant frequency readings are taken for diphthongs. Another notable exception is Beckford (1999), who examines onset, midpoint, and offset measurements.

Information extracted at vowel midpoint may not be as perceptually salient as information in the portions of the segment that show the greatest context effects, namely consonantal formant transitions at onset and offset. ʊtrange (1999: 163) summarizes the results of an earlier study (ʊtrange *et al.* 1979) thus: "... vowels produced in several CVC contexts were identified more accurately than vowels produced in isolation (#V#) by the same panel of talkers." ʊtrange (1999: 165) argues, in fact, that "... vowel targets in syllable centers are neither sufficient nor necessary for the accurate perception of coarticulated vowels." Ohala (1981: 189) also finds that

> some of the most important acoustic cues for primary place of articulation and certainly for secondary place of articulation are F_2 and F_3 transitions spreading from onset and offset of the consonant into preceding and following vowels and that such formant transitions may last 30–60 ms—that is, for a good proportion of the average vowel.

In light of the results reported by ʊtrange and her colleagues, it may be the case that the trend in sociophonetic work on American English vowel systems to rely on F_1 and F_2 measurements only at a single temporal location, usually described as the vowel nucleus (Labov 1994) or "steady state" (Fridland 2003) portion of the vowel, is problematic because these formant frequencies may not be as information-rich (perceptually) as portions of the signal which contain formant transitions associated with consonantal context effects. These formant transitions between vowels and consonants should also be examined.

6.2.1 Effects of following alveolar consonantal context on vowel spectra

As noted by ʊtevens (1998: 355), a constriction in the alveolar region causes a "... modest narrowing ... in the anterior or oral region and a widening in the posterior or pharyngeal region. The raising of the tongue tip to form a constriction causes a tapering of the area function behind the constriction point. . . . " When a high front vowel such as /i/ precedes an alveolar, the tongue body does not have to move far in order to make the constriction. According to ʊtevens, acoustically this event results in a slight downward movement for F_1 and F_2 (356). In contrast, a high back rounded vowel such as /u/ differs from its front counterpart for F_2 values and tongue body position (356). /u/ is produced with a "narrowing in the pharyngeal region," and one acoustic consequence of this configuration is a low F_2 value (356). The constriction is moved from a backed position toward a more fronted position in the oral cavity in order to execute an alveolar consonant, which has a relatively high F_2 value (Johnson 2003: 143).

Fronting of pre-alveolar /u/ is likely in part the result of context effects on the vowel from the following consonant. The overall pre-alveolar F_2 distances for /u/ and /i/ were smaller than those for the other contexts: 480 Hz (AA) and 389 Hz (AP) at midpoint and 597 Hz (AA) and 540 Hz (AP) at offset (Table 6.1). Vowel duration is an important factor to consider in discussions of context effects from the following consonant on vowel quality. ʊtevens (1998: 572) notes that tongue body movement from a back vowel into a fronted position such as that necessary for the production of an alveolar takes about 100 ms. He also points out that vowels which are less than 200–300 ms may show coarticulatory effects from adjacent consonants throughout their duration. The overall mean duration of 144 ms for pre-alveolar tokens of /u/ (Table 6.11) suggests that context effects

Table 6.11   Duration of /u/ and /ʊ/ (in ms) by ethnicity in the pre-alveolar context

Ethnicity	Vowel	Mean	Stdev	N
AA	/u/	148	64	97
	/ʊ/	136	86	75
	Total	143	74	172
AP	/u/	135	43	43
	/ʊ/	119	68	36
	Total	127	56	79
Total	/u/	144	58	140
	/ʊ/	131	81	111
	Total	138	69	251

from the following alveolar consonant at both midpoint and offset are a reasonable explanation for fronting of /u/ in this environment. F_2 values must rise as the articulators move into position to form a constriction for an alveolar consonant, and it is possible that the following contextual effects have an impact on vowel quality at least as early as midpoint.

Lower-high vowels such as /ʊ/and/ɪ/ show acoustic patterns similar to /u/ and /i/, respectively, when the articulators move into position to execute an alveolar consonant (ʊtevens 1998: 282). The overall pre-alveolar F_2 distances for /ʊ/ and /ɪ/ were 275 Hz (AA) and 219 Hz (AP) at midpoint and 219 Hz (AA) and 87 Hz (AP) at offset. For /ʊ/, the overall pre-alveolar mean duration was 131 ms, hence context effects on /ʊ/from the following alveolar are probable at both midpoint and offset. Pre-alveolar /u/ and /ʊ/ glide toward the back of the vowel envelope rather than toward the front for nearly all of the speakers; the front-back differences are larger at offset than midpoint because there is a decrease in F_2 for back vowels at offset. I will return to this issue in the discussion of the combined effects of backing and rounding in ʊection 6.3.

6.2.2 Effects of following labial consonantal context on vowel spectra

The overall pre-labial F_2 distances for /u/ and /i/ were 1374 Hz (AA) and 1107 Hz (AP) at midpoint and 1388 Hz (AA) and 1172 Hz (AP) at offset (Table 6.1). The distance measures between /i/ and /u/ are much greater in pre-labial contexts at both midpoint (AA 1374 Hz, AP 1107 Hz) and offset (AA 1388 Hz, AP 1172 Hz) than in pre-alveolar (midpoint: AA 480 Hz, AP 389 Hz; offset: AA 597 Hz, AP 540 Hz) and word-final (midpoint: AA 700 Hz, AP 620 Hz; offset: AA 859 Hz, AP 945 Hz). A greater F_2 distance measure indicates a more backed variant of /u/. The phonetic characteristics of the labial environment tend to inhibit fronting. Labial consonants show low values for F_2 and back vowels do as well. ʊtevens (1998: 341) describes both labials and back vowels as showing close spacing of the first two formants and notes that the F_2 movement of a back vowel into a labial consonant is small (341). The articulatory configuration of a back vowel such as /u/ can be modeled by two coupled tubes (one corresponding to the front cavity and one to the back) "... with the closely spaced first two formants associated roughly with these two sections" (342). There is little movement necessary when a back vowel transitions into a labial consonant (and vice versa) because the " . . . low-frequency back-cavity resonance remains almost unchanged as the labial constriction changes the front-cavity resonance" (342). Context effects on /u/ from the following labial consonant account for the relative backness of these variants for both southern migrant groups as compared to pre-alveolar tokens. The mean durations for pre-labial tokens were 156 ms (AA) and 128 ms (AP), values small enough to allow for potential influence from adjacent consonants through a large percentage of the segment (Stevens 1998).

6.2.3 Word-final context

The patterning of word-final variants suggests that context effects from the following consonant are conditioning the fronting of /u/ rather than fronting being the result of speakers aiming at an intentional vowel target. Overall F_2 distances for word-final /u/ and /i/ (Table 6.1) were 700 Hz (AA) and 620 Hz (AP) at midpoint and 859 Hz (AA) and 945 Hz (AP) at offset. These distance values between front and back counterparts fall between those reported for the pre-alveolar and pre-labial contexts, providing further support for an explanation for patterns of fronting and backing which appeals to following context effects. Alveolar environments promote fronting, and labial ones inhibit it—both for the AA and AP groups; it makes sense that the F_2 of final vowels, which show no following contextual effects, falls between these two extremes.

6.2.4 Effects of following velar consonantal context on vowel spectra

Recall that this environment was not included in the analysis of /u/ due to an insufficient number of tokens. The overall pre-velar distance measures (F_2 distances between /ʊ/ and /ɪ/, Table 6.2) were 560 Hz (AA) and 832 Hz (AP) at midpoint and 552 Hz (AA) and 817 Hz (AP) at offset. Note that the F_2 differences between midpoint and offset are slight, and that the distances are several times larger than the pre-alveolar distances of 275 Hz (AA) and 219 Hz (AP) at midpoint and 219 Hz (AA) and 87 Hz (AP) at offset. The mean durations for each group are 105 ms (AA) and 101 ms (AP), values which are low enough for there to be coarticulation between the vowel and the following consonant at least as early as midpoint (ʊtevens 1998). The phonetic characteristics of velars are described below.

ʊtevens discusses important differences for velars with respect to alveolars and labials: the position of the constriction is farther from the lips, the length of the constriction is greater for a velar than it is for an alveolar or labial, and the rate of change (increase or decrease) of the cross-sectional area at the closure is less for a velar than it is for an alveolar or a labial (1998: 365). In order to form a velar, the tongue body is raised to form a closure against the soft palate or the posterior portion of the hard palate (365). The lowest resonant frequency of the cavity which is in front of the constriction will be associated with either F_2 or F_3, and one of the resonant frequencies of the back cavity will be "relatively close" to the front-cavity resonance. This configuration results in a proximity of F_2 and F_3 (365–366), the well-known "velar pinch." In addition, ʊtevens notes that the spectrum amplitude of the peak for a velar is "comparable" to that of the F_2 value of the following vowel (373). ʊpecifically, there is " ... considerable variability in the position of the constriction depending on the front-back tongue position of the (flanking) vowel ... " (374). Thus, a velar consonant shows a more fronted tongue body position (and thus a higher F_2 value) when flanked by a front vowel such as /ɪ/ than for a back vowel such as /ʊ/ (374).

As noted above, the mean durations for this environment are sufficiently small enough for there to be context effects from the following consonant at least as early as midpoint for both ʊouthern migrant groups. The phonetic characteristics of velars which are reviewed above make it clear that a velar constriction following a back vowel inhibits fronting. Both the AP and the AA groups show backing for this variant, and context effects from the following consonant are a reasonable explanation for this pattern.

6.2.5 Summary

Context effects on preceding vowels play a role in the fronting of the pre-alveolar variants of /u/ and /ʊ/ and in the backing of pre-labial /u/ and pre-velar /ʊ/. Formant values for word-final variants expectedly fall in the middle, suggesting that fronting is conditioned by following consonantal context rather than resulting from an intentional vowel target. As noted above, context effects are expected to follow lawful and predictable paths as they progress through varieties.

However, varieties may show differences in rates of changes which are conditioned by context effects. For the most part, the AA and AP groups show strikingly similar context effects on fronting from the following consonant. The only ethnic difference for context effects is that the AA group shows a smaller /ʊ/~/ɪ/ F_2 distance (i.e. more fronting) for the pre-alveolar variant than the AP group. As noted above, the context effects of velars following a back vowel inhibit fronting. The AP group, then, shows greater context effects from the following consonant for this variant than the AA group although both groups show less fronting for this variant than for the pre-alveolar variant. Average durations of these vowels are short enough to allow following contextual effects at least as early as midpoint.

6.3   Rounding and backing

As shown in ʊection 6.1, both ethnicities have fronted pre-alveolar variants of /u/ and /ʊ/. ʊo far I have discussed the distances in F_2 values between front and back counterparts in terms of fronting versus backing. However, there is another factor, rounding, which by adding length to the vocal tract can also influence F_2 values. Lip rounding and backing of the tongue body both lower F_2 and can be implemented independently or simultaneously. One-way differentiation between phonologically front and back vowels and between fronted and backed variants of /u/ and /ʊ/ can therefore be achieved is through a combination of rounding and backing. ʊtevens describes how rounding and a backed tongue body position can work together to achieve a more robust acoustic effect for /u/: " . . . a stable acoustic characteristic for a high back vowel with a maximally low F_2 can best be achieved by rounding the lips as well as displacing the tongue body backward . . . " (1998: 279–280). ʊtevens describes how a fronted tongue body position raises F_2 values:

> As the tongue body is displaced forward while maintaining a narrowing in the lower pharynx, the frequency of the second formant will increase to a maximum value when the configuration is such that the natural frequency of the short section consisting of the larynx tube and the lower pharynx becomes roughly equal to the second natural frequency of the remainder of the vocal tract anterior to the constricted pharyngeal region. (ʊtevens 1998: 276)

Lip rounding and a backed tongue body position can thus enhance one another in order to differentiate the high back vowel /u/ from its front counterpart /i/. ʊtevens (1998: 282–283) and Ladefoged (1996: 131–134) describe the semi-high vowel /ʊ/ as showing similar acoustic patterns of tongue body displacement and rounding as /u/, although the degree of rounding is less than that for /u/. Rounding also lowers F_2 (ʊtevens 1998: 292). Conversely, spreading of the lips, along with fronting the tongue body, results in an increase in F_2. Because rounding and backing have the same acoustic effect of lowering F_2, it is not possible to determine their relative magnitudes from acoustic data alone. It is possible that the fronted variants of /u/ and /ʊ/ are realized through unrounding of the canonically rounded back variants, through tongue body movement alone (in which case they remain rounded), or through a combination of the gestures of both the tongue body and the lips. The question of how speakers produce these variants thus remains open for future research that incorporates articulatory data.

6.4 Nguyen's (2006) real-time analysis of /ʊ/ by social status for Detroit African Americans and Nguyen and Anderson's (2006) comparisons of /ʊ/ fronting among African American and Midwestern Whites in the Detroit area

Nguyen (2006) analyzed /ʊ/ fronting for both contemporary Detroit AAE data and a subset of ʊhuy, Wolfram, and Riley's Detroit AAE corpus collected in 1966. ʊhe examined fronting differences between velar and alveolar tokens of /ʊ/ by social status. Her results show that, for the 1966 corpus, only the higher status speakers have a context-based difference in fronting, while among contemporary speakers, this context difference has spread across the whole social status spectrum. More specifically, both the 1966 high-status speakers and contemporary speakers of all social status levels show context-based patterns of fronting for /ʊ/ in which pre-alveolar tokens are significantly more fronted than pre-velar tokens, the same pattern of phonetic conditioning reported for my results above. Nguyen high-lights that the effect of social status on fronting has changed over time, a change which was also sensitive to phonetic conditioning: " . . . high status speakers fronted pre-alveolar tokens /ʊ/ significantly more than they fronted pre-velar tokens, and more than low status speakers fronted in either context" (2006: 153). Nguyen claims that high back vowel fronting is a change in progress in Detroit AAE, her results " . . . show(ing) that pre-alveolar and pre-velar /ʊ/ are differently correlated with social categories and even change differently over time, suggesting that /ʊ/ fronting is a change in progress rather than a completed change" (166). Further, women appear to be leading the change; contemporary women show more fronting than both the 1966 female speakers and more fronting than men in either year of recording (162). The most relevant pattern from Nguyen's analysis of /ʊ/ fronting in real time and with regard to social status for the current study is that her results, like those reported in this volume, show very strong phonetic context effects. ʊhe offers the following summary of the interaction of context effects, social status of speakers, and change over time:

> The pre-alveolar contexts appear to have undergone a change; in 1966, the highest status speakers had /ʊ/ values that were much more fronted in pre-alveolar contexts than pre-velar contexts, while the lowest status speakers equally backed pre-alveolar and pre-velar /ʊ/ values. Among contemporary speakers, this status difference has disappeared and the difference between the pre-alveolar and pre-velar /ʊ/ is nearly as large among all (contemporary Detroit AAE) speakers as it was only among high status speakers in 1966. (152)

Nguyen's detailed analysis of change over time in Detroit AAE lends support to my claim that high-back vowel fronting is phonetic in nature—governed by coarticulatory context effects. ʊpecifically, pre-alveolar contexts promote fronting for both /u/ and /ʊ/, a good example of anticipatory coarticulation. I will argue in Chapter 8 that many phonetic changes are contextually conditioned, at least in the early stages of change.

Nguyen (2006) did not analyze /u/. However, Nguyen and Anderson (2006) compare patterns of fronting for both /u/ and /ʊ/ for six contemporary Detroit AA and Detroit White speakers. Echoing the results reported for the current study as well as for Nguyen (2006), we found that patterns of fronting were also contextually conditioned for the six White speakers in the study.

Table 6.12 F$_2$ measurements of /ʊ/ tokens among Detroit White female speakers (Nguyen and Anderson 2006)

	N	F2 at midpoint	Stdev at midpoint	F2 at offset	Stdev at offset
Pre-alveolar	112	1644	279	1692	268
Pre-velar	39	1362	205	1379	191
Difference		282**		313**	

** These context-based differences are significant at a level of $p < 0.001$.

ʋimilar to Nguyen (2006) and to the current study, the tokens of /ʊ/ that are analyzed by Nguyen and Anderson (2006) are restricted to two following contexts: pre-alveolar and pre-velar. While this vowel does occur in other contexts, tokens of these lexical items occur too infrequently to be included. Our primary research question was whether or not there is a difference in following context for these vowels among White speakers in Detroit area. Table 6.12 provides the F2 means for White speakers by following context.

The "difference" total in the last row of Table 6.12 is the difference in Hz between the average measurement of pre-alveolar and pre-velar tokens at each respective point of measurement. These significance levels were found using *t*-tests, or univariate statistical tests. Using a distance measure renders normalization unnecessary and allows for quantitative comparisons across individual speakers as well as groups. The bar graph in Figure 6.4 provides a visual display of the data in Table 6.12.

Table 6.12 and Figure 6.4 show that pre-alveolar tokens show higher F2 values than the pre-velar tokens at both midpoint and offset. The next level of analysis for Nguyen and Anderson compared the contextual differences for /ʊ/ fronting for the White speakers to that of contemporary AA speakers.

Context-based difference in /ʊ/ fronting is greater at the offset than at the midpoint. This is the expected pattern because the offset measure is closer to the actual following consonant and is thus expected to show greater coarticulatory context effects. Table 6.13 shows that /ʊ/ fronting measures differ significantly by context for each of the three groups included. The context-based difference, however, appears to be somewhat smaller for contemporary AA

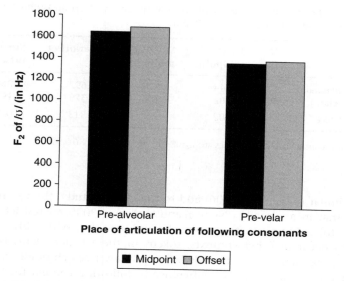

Figure 6.4 F$_2$ measurements of /ʊ/ tokens among White speakers (Nguyen and Anderson 2006)

Table 6.13 /ʊ/ Comparisons between Detroit White and Detroit African American participants (Nguyen and Anderson 2006)

	N	F$_2$ at midpoint	Stdev at midpoint	F$_2$ at offset	Stdev at offset
White speakers					
Pre-alveolar	112	1644	279	1692	268
Pre-velar	39	1362	205	1379	191
Difference		282**		313**	
African American Speakers – Contemporary					
Pre-alveolar	191	1515	273	1561	276
Pre-velar	93	1275	204	1305	211
Difference		240**		256**	
African American Speakers – 1966					
Pre-alveolar	182	1476	247	1515	241
Pre-velar	69	1328	196	1298	190
Difference		148**		217**	

** These context-based differences are significant at a level of $p < 0.001$.

Table 6.14 Results from a multivariate model, with examination of interactions between speaker group and following context while controlling for individual speaker effects and preceding place of articulation (Nguyen and Anderson 2006)

Predictor	Midpoint significance level	Offset significance level
Intercept	0.000	0.000
Preceding place of articulation	0.000	0.000
Following place of articulation	0.000	0.000
Speaker group	0.071	0.388
Preceding place * Speaker group	0.000	0.000
Following place * Speaker group	0.003	0.072

"Speaker group" refers to three groups—White speakers, contemporary AA speakers, and 1966 AA speakers.

speakers, and smaller yet for the 1966 speakers, than the context-differences for White speakers. The actual extent to which context-based /ʊ/ fronting differs across the three groups can be better assessed by a multivariate model, which has the power to allow examination of interactions between speaker group and following context while controlling for individual speaker effects and preceding place of articulation.

Table 6.14 shows that two interaction terms were included in each statistical model. They test whether the preceding place of articulation and the following place of articulation have a different effect on production patterns across speaker groups. The significance levels indicate that they do (with the exception of the following place for speaker group at the offset at $p = 0.072$).

Nguyen and Anderson (2006) focused particularly on the differences for following place of articulation. Context has a significantly different effect on different groups at the midpoint measure, and approaches a significant difference at the offset measure. Our next question, then, was: What differing effect does context have across these groupsɑ In other words, which speaker group's /ʊ/ fronting is more and less affected by the following contextɑ

The line graphs in Figures 6.5 and 6.6 show F2 measures by following place of articulation and speaker group.

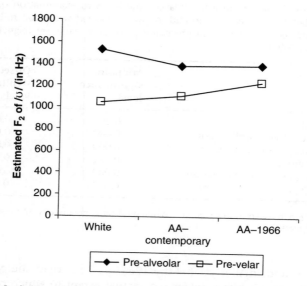

Figure 6.5 /ʊ/ F$_2$ estimated coefficients at onset (Nguyen and Anderson 2006)

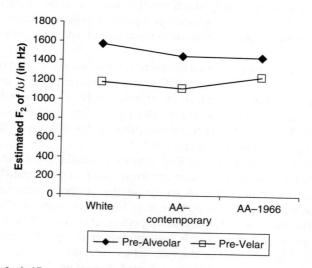

Figure 6.6 /ʊ/ F$_2$ estimated coefficients at offset (Nguyen and Anderson 2006)

Table 6.15 Estimated coefficients that result from the multivariate analysis (Nguyen and Anderson 2006)

Group	Difference at midpoint	Difference at offset
White	480	396
AA—Contemporary	276	334
AA—1966	155	207

Table 6.15 presents estimated coefficients that result from the multivariate analysis. In this analysis, the group of White speakers serves as the baseline, with which the context-based difference of AA speakers is compared.

Figure 6.7 is a bar graph, displaying the estimated mean differences in Table 6.15. As mentioned above, the multivariate models for /ʊ/ fronting indicated that the following context at vowel offset had different effects on the three speaker groups included in Nguyen and Anderson (2006).

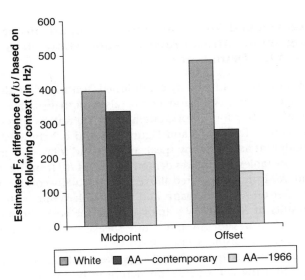

Figure 6.7 Estimates of context-based differences in /ʊ/ fronting (Nguyen and Anderson 2006)

From the tables and figures above, it is clear that in the Detroit area, White speakers have a greater context-based difference than contemporary AA speakers, who, in turn, have a greater context-based difference than AAs from 1966.

A very clear picture of context-based fronting of /ʊ/ emerges in the comparison between Nguyen (2006), Nguyen and Anderson (2006), and the current study. To summarize the patterns: Nguyen (2006) reports context-based fronting for Wolfram's 1966 middle-class Detroit AA speakers in which pre-alveolar tokens are more fronted than pre-velar ones. The same pattern holds for her contemporary sample of Detroit AAs spanning the entire social status spectrum. The current study reports the same pattern for both Detroit AA southern migrant participants as well as AP southern migrant participants, and Nguyen and Anderson (2006) show that this pattern also exists in the speech of White Detroiters. /ʊ/ fronting may be unrelated across the different communities in the Detroit area, or it may be a result of dialect contact. The question may be resolved by examining the patterns of fronting among Wolfram's 1966 White speakers, which is open for future research.

6.5   Nguyen and Anderson's (2006) comparisons of /u/ fronting among African American and Midwestern Whites in the Detroit area

In addition to the contextually conditioned fronting of /ʊ/ discussed above, Nguyen and Anderson (2006) also compare context-based patterns of fronting for /u/ for contemporary Detroit AA speakers and Detroit Whites. Table 6.16 and Figures 6.8 and 6.9 show F2 values at the midpoint and offset by speaker group and following phonetic context. The tables and figures demonstrate that /u/ fronting, like the results for /ʊ/ fronting reported above, is contextually conditioned for both the Detroit AA participants and the Detroit White participants.

The results of four ANOVA analyses, one for both the midpoint and offset measures for AA and White speakers, along with Scheffe post-hoc tests, are displayed in Table 6.17.

Table 6.17 shows that among AA speakers, tokens with all three types of following consonants are significantly different from one another. Among White speakers, however, pre-labial tokens are significantly less fronted than tokens in other contexts; however, at both

Table 6.16 Following places of articulation for /u/ F_2 by ethnic group (Nguyen and Anderson 2006)

	N	Midpoint	Offset
African American			
Word boundary	130	1868	1693
Labial	35	1060	1051
Alveolar	95	2065	1916
White			
Word boundary	68	1859	1753
Labial	25	1296	1301
Alveolar	22	1897	1805

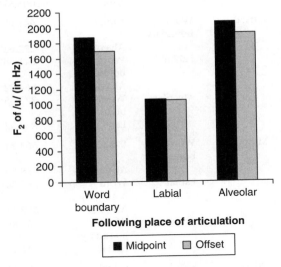

Figure 6.8 Mean African American /u/ F_2 measures at midpoint and offset for word boundary, labial, and alveolar following contexts (Nguyen and Anderson 2006)

midpoint and offset, the pre-word boundary and pre-alveolar tokens do not differ significantly from one another.

Finally, multivariate analyses, in which following place of articulation, speaker ethnicity, and the interaction of these two predictors are

Table 6.17 The results of four ANOVA analyses, one for both the midpoint and offset measures for African American and White speakers, along with Scheffe post-hoc tests (Nguyen and Anderson 2006)

Ethnicity	Dependent variable	Following place	Following place	Mean difference (I–J)	Sig.
African American	Midpoint	Word boundary	Labial	808.89*	0.000
		Labial	Alveolar	−196.68*	0.002
			Word boundary	−808.89*	0.000
		Alveolar	Alveolar	−1005.57*	0.000
			Word boundary	196.68*	0.002
			Labial	1005.57*	0.000
	Offset	Word boundary	Labial	641.68*	0.000
		Labial	Alveolar	−222.65*	0.001
			Word boundary	−641.68*	0.000
		Alveolar	Alveolar	−864.32*	0.000
			Word boundary	222.65*	0.001
			Labial	864.32*	0.000
White	Midpoint	Word boundary	Labial	563.24*	0.000
		Labial	Alveolar	−38.89	0.894
			Word boundary	−563.24*	0.000
		Alveolar	Alveolar	−602.13*	0.000
			Word boundary	38.89	0.894
			Labial	602.13*	0.000
	Offset	Word boundary	Labial	451.61*	0.000
		Labial	Alveolar	−52.34	0.822
			Word boundary	−451.61*	0.000
		Alveolar	Alveolar	−503.95*	0.000
			Word boundary	52.34	0.822
			Labial	503.95*	0.000

* The mean difference is significant at the 0.05 level.

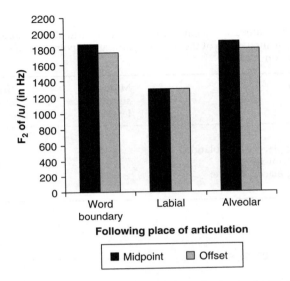

Figure 6.9 Mean White /u/ F$_2$ measures at midpoint and offset for word boundary, labial, and alveolar following contexts (Nguyen and Anderson 2006)

included for each point of measurement, yield the results presented in Table 6.18.

The significance levels in Table 6.18 indicate that following place of articulation is a highly significant predictor of /u/ fronting. Speakers' ethnicity, however, is less a significant predictor; it appears that at both midpoint and offset measures, the difference between AA and White speakers is accounted for by the differing effects that the following place of articulation has on each group. At midpoint and offset, the effect of the following context is significantly different for speaker group. To illustrate how the different speaker groups are affected by the following contexts, Nguyen and Anderson (2006) present the graphs (Figures 6.10 and 6.11) of the estimated marginal means that result from the multivariate analyses.

Nguyen and Anderson (2006) demonstrate that the multivariate models, like the earlier descriptive statistics, show that pre-labial /u/ tokens are backed when compared to pre-word boundary and pre-alveolar tokens, and pre-alveolar tokens show the highest degree of fronting. Further, these graphs reveal that following place of

Table 6.18 Multivariate analysis testing place of articulation, speaker ethnicity, and the interaction of the two predictors at midpoint and offset (Nguyen and Anderson 2006)

Predictor	Midpoint significance level	Offset significance level
Intercept	0.000	0.000
Following place of articulation	0.000	0.000
Speaker ethnicity	0.690	0.214
Following place * Speaker ethnicity	0.013	0.050

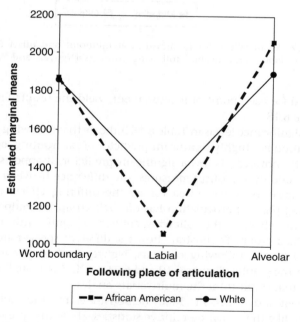

Figure 6.10 Estimated marginal means of /u/ F_2 measures at midpoint (Nguyen and Anderson 2006)

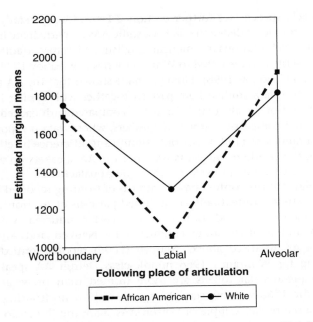

Figure 6.11 Estimated marginal means of /u/ F_2 measures at offset (Nguyen and Anderson 2006)

articulation has greater context effects on production of /u/ for AA speakers than for White speakers. In other words, at both places of measurements, AA speakers' pre-labial tokens are further back and pre-alveolar tokens further front than those produced by White speakers. Thus, the significant interaction of ethnicity and following context, found in both multivariate models, can be interpreted as following context having a *greater* effect on the /u/ tokens of AA speakers than on those of White speakers.

6.6 Conclusion

Using systematic spectral measures taken at vowel midpoint and offset, and using methods and statistical techniques sensitive to vowel context, I have found fronted variants of /u/ and /ʊ/ for all six of the AA speakers analyzed here, a small-scale but robust counterexample to the common assertion that these variants characterize White, but not Black, speech (see further ʋection 2.1.4). More generally, these results provide evidence that at least some AAs do participate in widespread vowel rotations in American English, which have traditionally been described as restricted to White varieties (e.g. Labov 1994, 2001; Bailey and Thomas 1998). Finally, I have shown that the AA and AP production data studied here pattern together with similar fronted realizations of pre-alveolar /u/ and /ʊ/, compared with backed realizations of a comparison group of speakers, whose data is reported in Hillenbrand *et al.* (1995). The only significant difference by ethnicity among the ʋouthern migrants was that the AA speakers on average had a more fronted pre-velar/ʊ/ than the Appalachians.

ʋimilarly to the context-based patterns of fronting reported for the current study, contextually conditioned patterns of /ʊ/ fronting are also evident in the study of Detroit AA speech conducted by Nguyen (2006) and another study conducted by Nguyen and Anderson (2006). As discussed above, Nguyen (2006) reports context-based fronting for Wolfram's 1966 middle-class Detroit AA speakers in which pre-alveolar tokens are more fronted than pre-velar ones, while the 1966 working-class AA speakers show no fronting at all. Her contemporary sample of Detroit AAs spanning the entire social status spectrum shows the same pattern of contextually conditioned fronting in which pre-alveolar environments show more fronting than pre-velar environments. The current study reports the same pattern of contextually conditioned fronting of /ʊ/ for both Detroit AA ʋouthern migrant participants as well as AP ʋouthern migrant participants. Nguyen and Anderson (2006) show that this pattern also exists in the speech of White Detroiters.

Unfortunately, Nguyen (2006) did not analyze /u/. Patterns of /u/ fronting are also contextually conditioned in both the current study as well as those reported by Nguyen and Anderson (2006). For the Detroit AA and AP ʋouthern migrant participants in the current study, pre-alveolar /u/ is fronted relative to the position of pre-labial tokens of /u/, which are backed, and pre-word-boundary tokens, which fall in the middle of the two extremes of the front-back dimension of the vowel space. The same pattern is reported in Nguyen and Anderson (2006), which compares patterns of /u/ fronting for Detroit AA and Detroit White speakers; both groups of speakers show contextually-conditioned fronting in which pre-labial /u/ tokens are backed when compared to pre-word boundary and pre-alveolar tokens, and pre-alveolar tokens showing the highest degree of fronting. However, following place of articulation has greater context effects on production of /u/ for the Detroit AA speakers than for the Detroit White speakers. In other words, at both midpoint and offset, the AA participants showed pre-labial tokens further back and pre-alveolar tokens further front for the F_2 acoustic space than tokens produced by White speakers. In other words, following context has a *greater* effect on the /u/ tokens of AA speakers than on those of White speakers.

Contextually conditioned change progresses in an orderly fashion through environments: for example, pre-alveolar> pre-final> pre-labial for the fronting of /u/. Following environments whose acoustic and articulatory characteristics promote the change would show more advanced variants than environments which do not. For example, pre-alveolar contexts are amenable to fronting of the back vowels. Alveolar consonants are produced with a fronted tongue body; the acoustic consequence of this gesture is a high F_2. Back vowels, in contrast, show a backed tongue body and low F_2. The constriction must move forward in the front/back dimension of the articulatory space to produce an alveolar consonant after a back vowel. Labial consonants, which show a backed tongue body (and low F_2), inhibit fronting. The tongue body shows little or no movement going from a back vowel into a labial constriction.

For /ʊ/, it is not surprising (from a coarticulatory point of view) that pre-alveolar environments promote fronting while pre-velar environments inhibit it. A velar consonant shows a more fronted tongue body position (and thus a higher F_2 value) when flanked by a front vowel such as /ɪ/ than for a back vowel such as /ʊ/ (ʊtevens 1998: 374).

More generally, the results presented in this chapter suggest that context effects cannot be ignored in investigations of vowel variation and change in American English. Conversational data is produced rapidly, and coarticulation makes this motor activity fluent and efficient. Coarticulation binds articulatory gestures into words, phrases, narratives, and other speech events.

7
The Patterning of /ai/

/u/ and /ʊ/, discussed in Chapter 6, do not seem to be as socially salient as /ai/ in varieties of American English (see section 2.1.4). In this chapter I analyze speakers' productions of /ai/ and /ɑ/, both between groups and on a speaker-by-speaker basis. The first goal is to quantify diphthongization by comparing F_1 and F_2 movement in /ai/, which exhibits varying degrees of diphthongization, with F_1 and F_2 movement in /ɑ/, which is used as a reference because it is expected to be relatively monophthongal (Anderson 2003; forthcoming). The second goal is to determine to what extent, if any, the African American (AA) and Appalachian White (AP) speakers have similar patterns of diphthongization and glide-weakening for /ai/, and to determine the nature of the patterning in terms of voicing context. section 7.1 presents a group comparison that excludes the older speakers of each ethnicity. section 7.2 investigates the patterns for all speakers individually, including a comparison with a Midwestern White speaker, and section 7.3 summarizes the patterning of /ai/ for the AA participants in this study.

Chapter 2 reviewed the literature on the /ai/ diphthong and characterized it as socially salient. To summarize the patterns of realization for /ai/ that are relevant to this chapter, glide-weakening before voiceless consonants ("pre-voiceless contexts")—for example [la:t] "light," [sa:t] "sight"—is typically described as a more recent change (Thomas 2001: 37) restricted to some southern White varieties spoken in areas not part of the former plantation regions of the south, such as the smoky Mountains of Western North Carolina (Anderson 1998, 1999; Childs 2005) and rural areas of Texas (Thomas 2001: 133–160). The traditional pattern in which the /ai/ glide is weakened in pre-voiced and word-final contexts but robust in pre-voiceless contexts reported for the White varieties conservative for the /ai/ variable in the former plantation regions of the south is also the canonical pattern reported in the literature for AAE. Thomas (2001: 37) characterizes this pattern as "presumably older" than the pattern of glide-weakening in all phonetic contexts.

Although glide-weakening of /ai/ in the important pre-voiceless context is generally not considered to be a feature of AAE, recent reports suggest it is a change in progress in AAE. several recent studies of /ai/ in AAE report glide-weakening in the pre-voiceless context (Mallinson et al. 2001; Anderson 2002, 2003; Anderson and Fridland 2002; Fridland 2004; Childs 2005). The results presented in this chapter provide additional evidence that this change is not restricted to southern White varieties of English as is generally claimed. Indeed, I will argue in Chapter 8 that /ai/ glide-weakening in the pre-voiceless phonetic context appears to be a change in progress in Detroit AAE.

several different types of methods are utilized in variationist studies of /ai/. Impressionistic reports dominate sociolinguistic descriptions of /ai/ (Eckert 1996; Edwards 1997; schilling-Estes 2000; Anderson 1997, 2002, and others). These studies treat /ai/ in a binary fashion as either monophthongal or diphthongal. However, Thomas (2001) points out that the length of the glide varies considerably between fully diphthongal variants, nuclei with short offglides, and completely monophthongal variants, which suggests that potentially important gradient information may be missed if /ai/ is treated as a binary variable.

Methods for acoustic studies of /ai/ vary. Anderson's (1999) study of snowbird Cherokee English took F_1 and F_2 measurements at vowel midpoint and 25 ms from the end of the vowel offset. Thomas (2001) took measurements of the first two formants at "25 to 45 ms from the beginning of the vocoid for the nucleus and between 25 and 45 ms from the end of the glide" for non-Texas speakers. For the Texas speakers, his readings were taken " . . . in the center of steady states, or where F_2 changed trajectory if no steady state was present (but not closer than 25 ms to the end of the vocoid)" (12). Thomas (2000) investigated the effects of voicing on the first two formants of /ai/ and reported that measurements were taken from a window 45–25 ms before the end of the diphthong. For Wolfram and Thomas's (2002) study of Hyde County vowels, Thomas took F_1 and F_2 measurements from a 20 ms window at vowel midpoint for monophthongs and, for diphthongs, at 25–45 ms from the beginning as well as the end of the diphthong. Fridland (2004) took F_1 and F_2 measurements " . . . by examining LPC peaks, spectrograms, energy and pitch of the signal to determine . . . steady state or central tendency" and extracted "representative LPC values of both nuclear and glide segments. . . . " Fridland essentially looked at the signal displayed in a spectrogram to decide where to take her measurements: "ı enerally, glide readings were taken at the maximal point of expected glide direction before any following environmental transition." Unfortunately, not establishing precise temporal locations for measurements makes it difficult to replicate studies or to cross-compare results.

Although each of the acoustic studies described above reports varying degrees of diphthongization, none of them describes the length and direction of glide movement for F_1 and F_2 in a precise manner. For example, Fridland (2004) analyzes gradient variants of /ai/, but her methods of analyzing glide length and direction are based on impressionistic observations of spectrograms rather than a replicable procedure based on precise temporal locations in the signal. ʋhe categorized monophthongal tokens as those " . . . show(ing) only steady state readings throughout the segment," and claims to "fully account for the glide target range in the data" by examining two categories of "shortened glides." By visually inspecting the acoustic signal in a spectrogram, she tabulated "glide targets that fell between 100 and 200 Hertz of the nucleus" as "short" and "glide targets which had readings which fell within 100 Hertz of the nucleus" as "very short." ı lides which showed "much greater extension from the nucleus (300 to 500 Hertz)" were described as "full." One potential difficulty with this method is that measurements taken directly from a spectrogram display are not precise because of spectral smearing (Johnson 2003: 43–44). Although Fridland's work has much advanced the understanding of /ai/ glide-weakening in American English, she does not analyze or report whether tokens showed glide movement in F_1, F_2, or both and does not confirm her impressionistic interpretations of vowel plots with statistical results.

This chapter outlines a consistent procedure used to measure duration and identify temporal locations at which to take measurements for each token of /ai/. Movement in F_1 and F_2 from midpoint to offset is quantified, and the results are subjected to statistical analysis.

7.1 Comparison by ethnicity, vowel, and context

The differences between formant frequency measurements taken at midpoint and 25 ms before the end of the offset in F_1 and F_2 were calculated (see Chapter 5 for an account of the acoustic methods) for tokens of /ɑ/ and /ai/ from the four youngest speakers in the AP and AA groups. The two older speakers are excluded from this part of the analysis because the goal is to examine patterns of use by following phonetic context. The older speakers show a pattern of following voice conditioning for /ai/ glide-weakening while middle-aged and younger speakers do not. Although /ɑ/ is less diphthongal than /ai/, some movement in F_1 and F_2 is expected due to coarticulation with the following consonant. A completely glide-weakened or monoph-thongal /ai/ should show no more movement than /ɑ/, whereas a diphthongal /ai/ will show movement resulting from both phonetic context and some degree of movement into the second element of the diphthong (usually a low, mid, or high front vowel depending on the degree of weakening). Tables 7.1 and 7.2 show the change in Hz from midpoint to offset in F_1 and F_2 for both vowels, ethnicities, and voiced versus voiceless contexts.

Two GLM analyses of variance were conducted (for F_1 and F_2 move-ment) with three independent factors: vowel (/ɑ/ and /ai/), ethni-city (AA and AP), and context (voiced and voiceless). That different numbers of tokens were measured for the different combinations of vowels and environments is not a problem for the GLM procedure, which works with both balanced and unbalanced models. Tables 7.3 and 7.4 show the main effects for vowel, ethnicity, and context, and the interactions.

For F_1, the significant main effect for vowel ($p < 0.001$) shown in Table 7.3 demonstrates that movement for /ai/ (mean 139 Hz, stdev 141 Hz) was significantly greater than that for /ɑ/ (mean 68 Hz, stdev 133 Hz) overall. There was also a significant main effect for environ-ment ($p < 0.001$), with change from midpoint to offset for pre-voiced vowels (mean 125 Hz, stdev 145 Hz) being greater than that for pre-voiceless vowels (mean 92 Hz, stdev 136 Hz). Although there was no significant main effect for ethnicity, ethnicity had a significant

Table 7.1 F_1 movement (in Hz) from midpoint to offset for /ɑ/ and /ai/ by ethnicity and context. A positive value indicates raising

Ethnicity	Vowel	Context	Mean	Stdev	N
AA	/ɑ/	Voiced	91	148	113
		Voiceless	64	140	105
		Total	78	144	218
	/ai/	Voiced	164	141	135
		Voiceless	106	118	164
		Total	132	132	299
AP	/ɑ/	Voiced	69	113	110
		Voiceless	37	109	80
		Total	56	112	190
	/ai/	Voiced	160	148	120
		Voiceless	136	159	98
		Total	149	153	218
Total	/ɑ/	Voiced	80	132	223
		Voiceless	53	128	185
		Total	68	131	408
	/ai/	Voiced	162	144	255
		Voiceless	117	135	262
		Total	139	141	517

interaction with vowel ($p < 0.05$), so it is necessary to investigate differences by ethnicity within vowels. The differences in F_1 movement by ethnicity within vowels can be seen in Table 7.5, which shows the estimated marginal means for the interactions of these factors. Movement for /ai/ is not significantly different by ethnicity, as the mean AA movement falls within the 95% confidence interval of the mean AP movement, and vice versa. For /ɑ/, the AA mean of 77 Hz, with the confidence interval [59, 95], is higher than the AP mean of 53 Hz (C.I. [34, 73]). Although each group's mean is beyond the other group's interval, the AA group's lower bound of 59 Hz is exceeded by the AP's upper bound of 73 Hz. The difference between the group means (24 Hz) is thus not very substantial. The interesting result for this study, however, is not the (slight) difference in F_1 for /ɑ/ by environment and ethnicity, but rather the lack of a difference in F_1 for /ai/.

For F_2, there was a significant main effect for vowel ($p < 0.001$), which means that overall movement for /ai/ (mean −179 Hz, stdev

Table 7.2 F_2 movement (in Hz) from midpoint to offset for /ɑ/ and /ai/ by ethnicity and context. A negative value indicates fronting

Ethnicity	Vowel	Context	Mean	Stdev	N
AA	/ɑ/	Voiced	−59	223	113
		Voiceless	−46	143	105
		Total	−53	189	218
	/ai/	Voiced	−139	195	135
		Voiceless	−164	211	164
		Total	−153	204	299
AP	/ɑ/	Voiced	−29	195	110
		Voiceless	−33	179	80
		Total	−31	188	190
	/ai/	Voiced	−214	230	120
		Voiceless	−215	238	98
		Total	−215	233	218
Total	/ɑ/	Voiced	−44	210	223
		Voiceless	−40	160	185
		Total	−42	189	408
	/ai/	Voiced	−174	215	255
		Voiceless	−183	223	262
		Total	−179	219	517

218) was significantly greater than that for /ɑ/ (mean −47 Hz, stdev 187). There was no main effect for environment, nor did environment participate in any significant interactions. Voicing, therefore, does not appear to influence fronting, at least not on a group basis. Later, we will see that this does not hold for every individual. As with F_1, there was a significant interaction between vowel and ethnicity ($p < 0.01$). Estimated marginal means are shown as before in Table 7.6. In this case, the difference lies with /ai/ rather than /ɑ/. The AA group's mean of −52 Hz (C.I. [−80, −25]) is significantly less (in absolute value) than that of the AP group's mean of −215 Hz (C.I. [−242, −187]), which means that the AP group's /ai/ was overall more diphthongal in F_2 than the AA group's /ai/.

I also investigated differences in duration by ethnicity, vowel, and context. A GLM analysis showed significant interactions among all three of these factors ($F(1,908) = 4.322$, $p < 0.038$), with estimated marginal means shown in Table 7.7. In order from longest to shortest

Table 7.3 ANOVA of main effects and interactions for F_1 movement

Dependent variable: F_1 mid-off

Source	Type III sum of squares	df	Mean square	F	Sig.
ETHNICITY	6841.535	1	6841.535	0.374	0.541
VOWEL	1290306.553	1	1290306.553	70.592	0.000
CONTEXT	273902.455	1	273902.455	14.985	0.000
ETHNICITY * VOWEL	78018.610	1	78018.610	4.268	0.039
ETHNICITY * CONTEXT	11641.470	1	11641.470	0.637	0.425
VOWEL * CONTEXT	7675.967	1	7675.967	0.420	0.517
ETHNICITY * VOWEL * CONTEXT	22212.485	1	22212.485	1.215	0.271
Error	16761252.5	917	18278.356		
Total	29117204.0	925			
Corrected total	18390553.1	924			

Table 7.4 ANOVA of main effects and interactions for F_2 movement

Dependent variable: F_2 mid-off

Source	Type III sum of squares	df	Mean square	F	Sig.
ETHNICITY	96871.482	1	96871.482	2.303	0.129
VOWEL	4439337.901	1	4439337.901	105.544	0.000
CONTEXT	3754.814	1	3754.814	0.089	0.765
ETHNICITY * VOWEL	396369.467	1	396369.467	9.424	0.002
ETHNICITY * CONTEXT	623.095	1	623.095	0.015	0.903
VOWEL * CONTEXT	16876.140	1	16876.140	0.401	0.527
ETHNICITY * VOWEL * CONTEXT	24192.667	1	24192.667	0.575	0.448
Error	38570220.8	917	42061.309		
Total	56426033.0	925			
Corrected total	43399360.1	924			

Table 7.5 Estimated marginal means for F_1 midpoint-to-offset movement (in Hz) by ethnicity and vowel

Ethnicity	Vowel	Mean	Std. error	95% Confidence interval	
				Lower bound	Upper bound
AA	/ɑ/	77	9.163	59	95
	/ai/	135	7.856	119	150
AP	/ɑ/	53	9.933	34	73
	/ai/	148	9.204	130	166

Table 7.6 Estimated marginal means for F_2 movement by ethnicity and vowel

Ethnicity	Vowel	Mean	Std. error	95% Confidence interval	
				Lower bound	Upper bound
AA	/ɑ/	−52	13.900	−80	−25
	/ai/	−152	11.917	−175	−128
AP	/ɑ/	−31	15.068	−61	−1
	/ai/	−215	13.962	−242	−187

Table 7.7 Estimated marginal means for duration by ethnicity, vowel, and environment

Ethnicity	Vowel	Context	Mean	Std. error	95% Confidence interval	
					Lower bound	Upper bound
AA	/ɑ/	Voiced	181	6.634	168	194
		Voiceless	161	6.882	147	174
	/ai/	Voiced	222	6.069	210	234
		Voiceless	137	5.506	127	148
AP	/ɑ/	Voiced	141	6.723	127	154
		Voiceless	136	7.884	121	152
	/ai/	Voiced	157	6.754	144	171
		Voiceless	128	7.312	114	143

vowels, both groups have the same ranking: pre-voiced /ai/ > pre-voiced /ɑ/ > pre-voiceless /ɑ/ > pre-voiceless /ai/. There is a significant difference between the groups, however. For the AA group, each vowel is significantly shorter than the previous one in the list, with differences of 41 ms, 20 ms, and 24 ms, respectively. For the AP group, however, pre-voiceless /ɑ/ is not significantly shorter than pre-voiced /ɑ/ (5 ms), and pre-voiceless /ai/ is not significantly shorter than pre-voiceless /ɑ/ (8 ms). In other words, voicing context has much stronger conditioning effects on vowel duration for the AA group than for the AP group. Another contrast is that the AA group has significantly longer /ai/ in the pre-voiced environment (222 ms, C.I. [210, 234]) than the AP group (157 ms, C.I. [144, 171]), but not in the pre-voiceless environment, where the difference was only 9 ms. I do not have an explanation for these patterns and a more detailed analysis of duration is open for future analysis.

7.2 Speaker-by-speaker analysis

This section analyzes the ways in which individual speakers instantiate patterns of glide-weakening/diphthongization discussed in the previous section and in the literature. In mainstream varieties of American English, /ai/ is diphthongized across the board. In traditional southern White and AA varieties, /ai/ is glide-weakened in pre-voiced contexts and diphthongized in pre-voiceless contexts. In some AP and progressive southern White varieties, /ai/ is glide-weakened across the board. Table 7.8 summarizes these patterns.

7.2.1 Data overview

The dataset is the same as in the previous section, except for the inclusion of all six AA speakers and all six AP speakers. For each vowel, the relevant dependent variables are F_1 movement (F_1 frequency at midpoint minus that at offset) and F_2 movement (F_2 frequency at midpoint minus that at offset). In this speaker-by-speaker analysis, the independent variables are vowel (/ai/ or /ɑ/) and context (voiced or voiceless). Average movement, standard deviations, and n for each speaker in F_1 and F_2 are shown in Tables 7.9 (AA speakers) and 7.10 (AP speakers).

Table 7.8   Previously reported patterns of /ai/ glide-weakening in varieties of American English

	Pre-voiced /ai/ glide-weakening	Pre-voiceless /ai/ glide-weakening
Mainstream American English	No	No
Traditional Southern White	Yes	No
African American	Yes	Only recently reported*
Appalachian White	Yes	Yes
Progressive Southern White	Yes	Yes

* Anderson (2002, 2003); Anderson and Fridland (2002); Fridland (2004); Mallinson et al. (2001); Childs (2005).

7.2.2   Statistical analysis

For each speaker, two GLM analyses of variance were conducted, one for F_1 movement and one for F_2 movement, in order to test for main effects and interactions of vowel and context. In the discussion that follows, I report only the significant results.

7.2.2.1   Main effects

First, I discuss main effects for vowel. A significant main effect by vowel means that movement for /ai/ was significantly greater than that for /ɑ/ across phonetic contexts (voiced and voiceless). If there is no main effect for vowel and no significant interaction with context, then there was no significant difference at all in movement between /ai/ and /ɑ/. Such a speaker could be classified as showing across-the-board /ai/ glide-weakening. If there was no significant main effect but a significant interaction between vowel and context, then one has to examine vowels within voicing context and voicing context within vowels. Such interactions are examined later.

All speakers except for 1 (AA), 3 (AA), and 11 (AP) show a significant main effect for vowel in F_1 movement (Table 7.11). Speaker 1's F_1 values had significant interactions between vowel and voicing, which will be addressed later. F_1 movement for Speakers 3 and 11 had no significant interaction, so at this point we can conclude that for these two speakers there is no significant difference in F_1 movement between /ɑ/ and /ai/.

For F_2 movement, all speakers except 9 (AP) and 11 (AP) showed significant main effects of vowel, with more movement for /ai/ than

Table 7.9 Average F_1 and F_2 midpoint-to-offset movement (in Hz) by vowel and context for individual AA speakers

Speaker	Vowel	Context	F_1 movement			F_2 movement		
			Mean	**Stdev**	**N**	**Mean**	**Stdev**	**N**
1	/ɑ/	Voiced	127.39	131.741	18	−79.50	186.897	18
		Voiceless	61.11	110.370	9	61.67	135.156	9
		Total	105.30	126.925	27	−32.44	181.821	27
	/ai/	Voiced	80.94	79.739	31	−14.00	118.507	31
		Voiceless	126.97	96.111	39	−271.95	237.004	39
		Total	106.59	91.554	70	−157.71	231.723	70
2	/ɑ/	Voiced	58.19	80.173	37	20.41	172.069	37
		Voiceless	42.53	83.210	38	50.05	116.472	38
		Total	50.25	81.554	75	35.43	146.319	75
	/ai/	Voiced	158.81	97.647	53	−358.66	196.287	53
		Voiceless	200.90	83.746	68	−391.76	211.679	68
		Total	182.46	92.126	121	−377.26	204.903	121
3	/ɑ/	Voiced	48.65	136.866	17	5.35	140.514	17
		Voiceless	98.71	92.619	7	−67.00	89.327	7
		Total	63.25	125.735	24	−15.75	130.174	24
	/ai/	Voiced	93.96	107.416	24	−97.83	169.617	24
		Voiceless	72.33	101.816	40	−181.10	189.244	40
		Total	80.44	103.639	64	−149.88	185.268	64
4	/ɑ/	Voiced	93.76	113.259	21	−71.81	139.112	21
		Voiceless	60.39	126.155	46	−50.76	138.754	46
		Total	70.85	122.400	67	−57.36	138.159	67
	/ai/	Voiced	158.76	155.053	33	−119.45	174.965	33
		Voiceless	95.30	121.145	56	−200.75	226.117	56
		Total	118.83	137.350	89	−170.61	211.298	89
5	/ɑ/	Voiced	128.53	162.196	49	−88.39	278.117	49
		Voiceless	93.37	145.215	35	−41.37	137.627	35
		Total	113.88	155.423	84	−68.80	230.293	84
	/ai/	Voiced	194.33	159.821	33	−195.45	265.940	33
		Voiceless	147.08	142.839	38	−96.92	207.354	38
		Total	169.04	151.738	71	−142.72	239.806	71
6	/ɑ/	Voiced	44.35	137.131	26	−35.77	203.482	26
		Voiceless	.29	167.302	17	−32.35	189.140	17
		Total	26.93	149.436	43	−34.42	195.644	43
	/ai/	Voiced	183.02	119.616	45	−134.07	153.362	45
		Voiceless	117.73	77.040	30	−157.53	204.240	30
		Total	156.91	108.951	75	−143.45	174.546	75

Table 7.10 Average F_1 and F_2 midpoint-to-offset movement in Hz by vowel and context for individual AP speakers

Speaker	Vowel	Context	F_1 movement			F_2 movement		
			Mean	Stdev	N	Mean	Stdev	N
7	/ɑ/	Voiced	128.74	122.151	23	21.61	155.143	23
		Voiceless	50.00	125.733	25	33.96	149.181	25
		Total	87.73	128.984	48	28.04	150.565	48
	/ai/	Voiced	176.04	152.890	28	−43.54	168.868	28
		Voiceless	131.48	131.153	29	−48.48	164.502	29
		Total	153.37	142.744	57	−46.05	165.184	57
8	/ɑ/	Voiced	124.11	120.193	36	−51.03	210.904	36
		Voiceless	49.14	85.733	21	−66.67	164.884	21
		Total	96.49	113.952	57	−56.79	193.824	57
	/ai/	Voiced	257.05	186.023	22	−350.32	304.940	22
		Voiceless	152.30	164.711	23	−285.00	292.059	23
		Total	203.51	181.340	45	−316.93	296.851	45
9	/ɑ/	Voiced	35.67	107.090	24	−117.83	250.100	24
		Voiceless	53.07	152.010	15	−39.27	245.914	15
		Total	42.36	124.611	39	−87.62	248.271	39
	/ai/	Voiced	147.78	101.246	23	−188.52	196.279	23
		Voiceless	159.36	201.613	33	−161.58	236.655	33
		Total	154.61	166.682	56	−172.64	219.486	56
10	/ɑ/	Voiced	22.83	95.394	29	8.24	128.129	29
		Voiceless	12.92	93.047	25	0.16	115.789	25
		Total	18.24	93.557	54	4.50	121.494	54
	/ai/	Voiced	122.41	113.311	54	−204.93	204.811	54
		Voiceless	140.48	130.910	23	−243.00	243.199	23
		Total	127.81	118.254	77	−216.30	216.059	77
11	/ɑ/	Voiced	31.11	119.467	18	−53.28	141.340	18
		Voiceless	11.75	114.457	20	45.20	99.188	20
		Total	20.92	115.676	38	−1.45	129.282	38
	/ai/	Voiced	15.76	120.567	17	−38.24	158.657	17
		Voiceless	2.29	93.267	21	−75.90	90.028	21
		Total	8.32	105.044	38	−59.05	125.007	38
12	/ɑ/	Voiced	77.19	90.596	21	58.95	122.222	21
		Voiceless	43.26	115.376	19	−35.05	208.134	19
		Total	61.07	103.186	40	14.30	172.959	40
	/ai/	Voiced	168.24	184.073	21	−124.05	180.652	21
		Voiceless	71.42	60.039	19	−189.16	127.694	19
		Total	122.25	146.414	40	−154.98	159.204	40

Table 7.11 Main effects of vowel on F_1 and F_2 midpoint-to-offset movement

Ethnicity	Speaker	df	F_1 movement		F_2 movement	
			F	Sig.	F	Sig.
AA	1	(1,96)	0.167	0.684	9.033	0.003
	2	(1,195)	101.958	0.000	226.449	0.000
	3	(1,87)	0.110	0.741	6.101	0.016
	4	(1,155)	5.064	0.026	10.014	0.002
	5	(1,154)	5.750	0.018	4.605	0.033
	6	(1,117)	28.451	0.000	9.670	0.002
AP	7	(1,104)	5.987	0.016	5.525	0.021
	8	(1,101)	16.821	0.000	26.946	0.000
	9	(1,94)	11.278	0.001	3.779	0.055
	10	(1,130)	31.582	0.000	45.002	0.000
	11	(1,75)	0.233	0.631	3.501	0.065
	12	(1,79)	4.699	0.033	21.275	0.000

for /ɑ/. Speaker 9 had no significant interactions, so vowel has no influence on her F_2 movement. Speaker 11 had a significant interaction for F_2 movement, to be addressed in the next section. In summary, all of the speakers either had a significant main effect of vowel in F_1 or F_2 movement, or had a significant interaction in F_1 or F_2. There was no speaker who had no main effect of vowel for F_1 and F_2 and no interaction, that is, no speaker for whom we can yet conclude that there was no difference whatsoever by vowel.

Table 7.12 summarizes the results for the main effect of voicing context, summing across /ai/ and /ɑ/. A significant main effect means that there was a significant overall difference in movement between voiced and voiceless contexts, regardless of the vowel. For F_1, five speakers had such effects (4, 6, 7, 8, and 12) and each of them had a greater midpoint-to-offset change in voiced contexts. These speakers' vowel plots are shown in Figures 7.1–7.5. Another five speakers' vowels (3, 5, 9, 10, and 11) showed no significant main effect and no interaction, so for these we can conclude that voicing context had no influence on movement for F_1, regardless of vowel. The vowels of Speakers 1 and 2 had no significant main effect, but a significant interaction, so raising varied with context in one vowel but not the other, to be examined later. For F_2, only Speaker 12's vowels showed a

Table 7.12 Main effects of voicing context on F_1 and F_2 midpoint-to-offset movement

Ethnicity	Speaker	df	F_1 movement		F_2 movement	
			F	Sig.	F	Sig.
AA	1	(1,96)	0.182	0.671	1.714	0.194
	2	(1,195)	1.061	0.304	0.004	0.950
	3	(1,87)	0.248	0.620	0.0130	0.081
	4	(1,155)	4.757	**0.031**	0.931	0.336
	5	(1,154)	2.734	0.100	3.689	0.057
	6	(1,117)	5.186	**0.025**	0.078	0.781
AP	7	(1,104)	5.488	**0.021**	0.014	0.906
	8	(1,101)	9.746	**0.002**	0.248	0.619
	9	(1,94)	0.199	0.657	1.130	0.291
	10	(1,130)	0.041	0.840	0.460	0.499
	11	(1,75)	0.408	0.525	1.151	0.287
	12	(1,79)	5.653	**0.020**	4.740	**0.033**

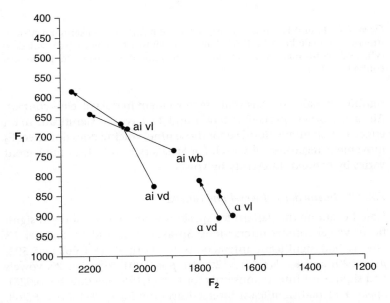

Figure 7.1 F_1 and F_2 values (in Hz) for /ɑ/ and /ai/ for Speaker 4, an African American female born in 1974. Arrows indicate midpoint-to-offset movement. Values are shown by voiced (vd), voiceless (vl), and word-final (wb) contexts. F_1 movement is greater in pre-voiced contexts

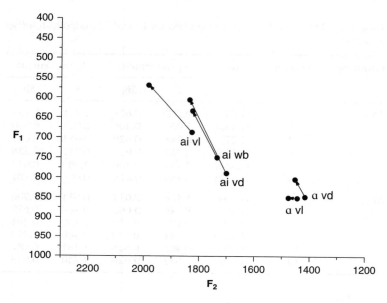

Figure 7.2 F_1 and F_2 values (in Hz) for /ɑ/ and /ai/ for Speaker 6, an African American female born in 1967. Values are shown by voiced (vd), voiceless (vl), and word-final (wb) contexts. F_1 movement is greater in pre-voiced contexts

significant main effect, with more movement in the voiceless context. All of the other speakers except 1 and 11 have no significant main effect and no interactions, so for those nine, voicing does not affect F_2 movement regardless of vowel. For Speakers 1 and 11, F_2 movement varies by context differently by vowel.

7.2.2.2   Interactions of vowel and context

Here I examine the pattern for speakers whose vowels showed significant vowel/context interactions: Speakers 1, 2, and 11. Speaker 1's vowels had significant interactions for both F_1 ($F(1,96) = 5.592$, $p < 0.020$) and F_2 ($F(1,96) = 20.016$, $p < 0.001$). Speaker 2's vowels had significant interactions only for F_1 ($F(1,195) = 5.069$, $p < 0.025$). Speaker 11 had significant interactions only for F_2 ($F(1,75) = 5.768$, $p < 0.019$). Tables 7.13–7.16 show estimated marginal means for movement by context and vowel.

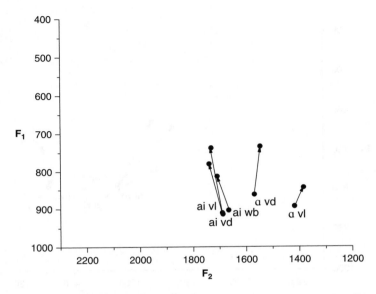

Figure 7.3 F_1 and F_2 values (in Hz) for /ɑ/ and /ai/ for Speaker 7, an Appalachian female born in 1931. Values are shown by voiced (vd), voiceless (vl), and word-final (wb) contexts. F_1 movement is greater in pre-voiced contexts

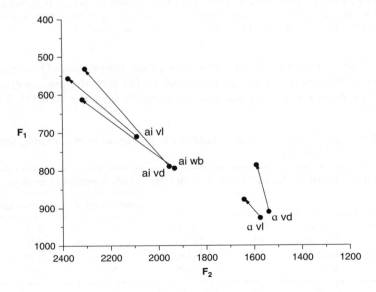

Figure 7.4 F_1 and F_2 values (in Hz) for /ɑ/ and /ai/ for Speaker 8, an Appalachian female born in 1960. Values are shown by voiced (vd), voiceless (vl), and word-final (wb) contexts. F_1 movement is greater in pre-voiced contexts

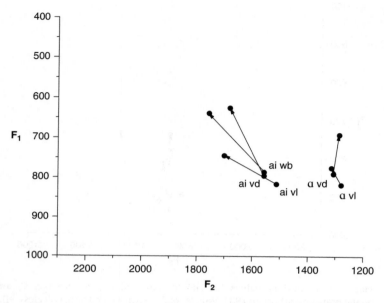

Figure 7.5 F_1 and F_2 values (in Hz) for /ɑ/ and /ai/ for Speaker 12, an Appalachian female born in 1965. Values are shown by voiced (vd), voiceless (vl), and word-final (wb) contexts. F_1 movement is greater in pre-voiced contexts. F_2 /ai/ movement is greater in pre-voiceless context

Table 7.13, for Speaker 1, shows that for /ɑ/, the pre-voiced F_1 movement was greater than the pre-voiceless. For /ai/, the pre-voiceless movement was greater, but not significantly, since the 95% C.I. for

Table 7.13   Estimated marginal means for F_1 movement by environment and vowel for Speaker 1

Vowel	Context	Mean (Hz)	Std. error (Hz)	95% Confidence interval	
				Lower bound	Upper bound
/ɑ/	Voiced	127	23.624	80	174
	Voiceless	61	33.410	-5	127
/ai/	Voiced	81	18.002	45	117
	Voiceless	127	16.049	95	159

Table 7.14 Estimated marginal means for F_2 movement by environment and vowel for Speaker 1

Vowel	Context	Mean (Hz)	Std. error (Hz)	95% Confidence interval	
				Lower bound	Upper bound
/ɑ/	Voiced	−80	44.371	−168	9
	Voiceless	62	62.750	−63	186
/ai/	Voiced	−14	33.811	−81	53
	Voiceless	−272	30.144	−332	−212

Table 7.15 Estimated marginal means for F_1 movement by environment and vowel for Speaker 2

Vowel	Context	Mean (Hz)	Std. error (Hz)	95% Confidence interval	
				Lower bound	Upper bound
/ɑ/	Voiced	58	14.303	30	86
	Voiceless	43	14.114	15	70
/ai/	Voiced	159	11.951	135	182
	Voiceless	201	10.550	180	222

Table 7.16 Estimated marginal means for F_2 movement by environment and vowel for Speaker 11

Vowel	Context	Mean (Hz)	Std. error (Hz)	95% Confidence interval	
				Lower bound	Upper bound
/ɑ/	Voiced	−53	29.019	−111	5
	Voiceless	45	27.530	−10	100
/ai/	Voiced	−38	29.861	−98	21
	Voiceless	−76	26.867	−129	−22

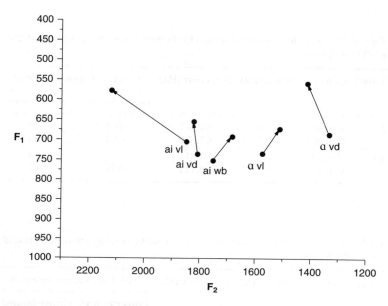

Figure 7.6 F_1 and F_2 values (in Hz) for /ɑ/ and /ai/ for Speaker 1, an African American female born in 1927. Values are shown by voiced (vd), voiceless (vl), and word-final (wb) contexts. /ai/ movement in F_1 and F_2 is greater in pre-voiceless context

the pre-voiced context, [45 Hz, 117 Hz], overlaps substantially with the interval for the pre-voiceless context, [95 Hz, 159 Hz]. The difference between pre-voiced and pre-voiceless /ai/ glide is especially great in F_2 (Table 7.14), where the pre-voiceless C.I. is [–332 Hz, –212 Hz] and pre-voiced is [–63 Hz, 186 Hz]. This speaker instantiates the traditional AAE pattern of pre-voiced glide-weakening and pre-voiceless diphthongization for /ai/, which can be seen in the vowel plot in Figure 7.6. Note the similarity in glide length of the pre-voiced and word-final environments compared to that of pre-voiceless /ai/.

Speaker 2's vowel interactions for F_1 are shown in Table 7.15, and her vowel plot in Figure 7.7. Although Speaker 2's movements for /ai/ are clearly longer than Speaker 1's overall (182 Hz versus 107 Hz in F_1, and –377 Hz versus –158 Hz in F_2), they have the same conditioning pattern of a longer glide in the pre-voiceless context, at least for F_1.

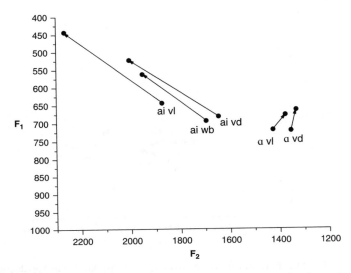

Figure 7.7 F$_1$ and F$_2$ values (in Hz) for /ɑ/ and /ai/ for Speaker 2, an African American female born in 1936. Values are shown by voiced (vd), voiceless (vl), and word-final (wb) contexts. /ai/ movement in F$_1$ is greater in pre-voiceless context

It is important to point out that Speaker 1 and Speaker 2 are older African American females (Speaker 1 was born in 1927; Speaker 2 was born in 1936). The traditional AA pattern of pre-voiced and pre-word boundary glide weakening and a robust glide in pre-voiceless contexts is expected due to the patterns reported in Anderson (2002). In that study, I found that middle-age and younger speakers showed pre-voiceless glide-weakening but that older speakers did not.

For Speaker 11 (Table 7.16), the significant F$_2$ difference by voicing occurs only for /ɑ/, so there is no difference in F$_2$ movement by context for /ai/. Note, however, that the absolute difference in Speaker 11's F$_2$ glide length for /ɑ/ is only 8 Hz (–53 Hz pre-voiced and 45 Hz pre-voiceless), but this is interpreted statistically as 98 Hz because the pre-voiceless variant glides backward and the pre-voiced one forward in the vowel space. Given the lack of a significant difference between /ɑ/ and /ai/ glide length and the lack of context effect on /ai/, this speaker fits the criteria for across-the-board glide-weakening, shown in the plot in Figure 7.8.

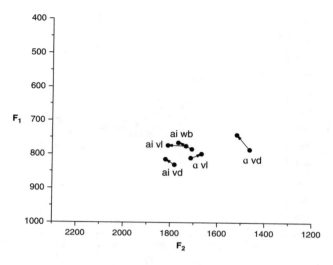

Figure 7.8 F_1 and F_2 values (in Hz) for /ɑ/ and /ai/ for Speaker 11 (an Appalachian female born in 1936), who shows across-the-board /ai/ glide-weakening. Values are shown by voiced (vd), voiceless (vl), and word-final (wb) contexts

Vowel plots for the remaining speakers 3 (AA), 5 (AA), 9 (AP), and 10 (AP) are shown below in Figures 7.9–7.12. These are the speakers who did not show significant contextual effects for F_1 or F_2 at the 0.05 level for either /ɑ/ or /ai/.

7.2.3   Comparison with a Midwestern White speaker

Table 7.17 and Figure 7.13 show /ɑ/ and /ai/ for Midwestern White Speaker 13. Recall that comparison with the data reported by Hillenbrand *et al.* (1995) is not possible, as they did not investigate /ai/. For F_1, a GLM analysis performed as before shows significant main effects for vowel ($F(1,102) = 10.616$, $p < 0.002$) and context ($F(1,102) = 11.707$, $p < 0.001$). This speaker has greater F_1 movement for /ai/ than /ɑ/ overall (192 Hz versus 65 Hz), and greater movement in pre-voiced contexts than pre-voiceless ones (109 Hz versus –32 Hz for /ɑ/ and 238 Hz versus 103 Hz for /ai/), presumably because the pre-voiced vowel is longer. There was no significant vowel by context interaction. For F_2, there was a significant main effect for vowel ($F(1,102) = 72.180$, $p < 0.001$), with the /ai/ midpoint-to-offset trajectory longer at –509 Hz compared to /ɑ/ at –12 Hz, and a significant interaction

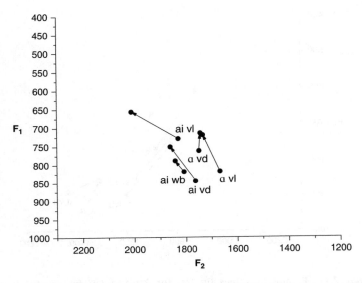

Figure 7.9 F$_1$ and F$_2$ values (in Hz) for /ɑ/ and /ai/ for Speaker 3, an African American female born in 1971. Values are shown by voiced (vd), voiceless (vl), and word-final (wb) contexts

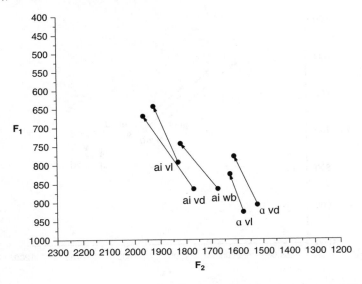

Figure 7.10 F$_1$ and F$_2$ values (in Hz) for /ɑ/ and /ai/ for Speaker 5, an African American female born in 1974. Values are shown by voiced (vd), voiceless (vl), and word-final (wb) contexts

124

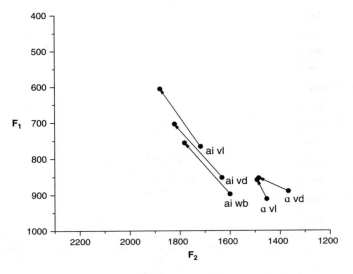

Figure 7.11 F$_1$ and F$_2$ values (in Hz) for /ɑ/ and /ai/ for Speaker 9, an Appalachian female born in 1951. Values are shown by voiced (vd), voiceless (vl), and word-final (wb) contexts

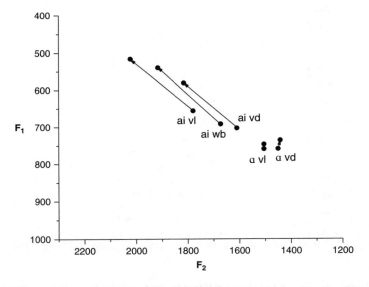

Figure 7.12 F$_1$ and F$_2$ values (in Hz) for /ɑ/ and /ai/ for Speaker 10, an Appalachian female born in 1949. Values are shown by voiced (vd), voiceless (vl), and word-final (wb) contexts

Table 7.17 Average F_1 and F_2 movement (in Hz) by vowel and context for Midwestern White Speaker 13

Vowel	Context	F_1 movement			F_2 movement		
		Mean	Stdev	N	Mean	Stdev	N
/ɑ/	Voiced	109	219	26	3	186	26
	Voiceless	−32	189	12	−45	180	12
	Total	65	218	38	−12	183	38
/ai/	Voiced	238	190	43	−575	291	43
	Voiceless	103	118	22	−381	242	22
	Total	192	180	65	−509	289	65

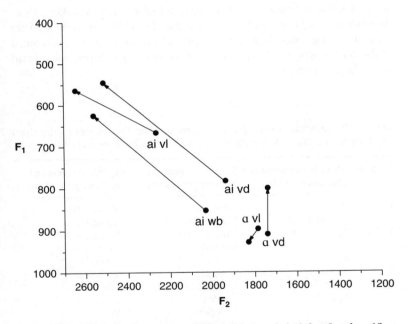

Figure 7.13 F_1 and F_2 values (in Hz) for /ɑ/ and /ai/ for Speaker 13, a Midwestern White female born in 1967. Values are shown by voiced (vd), voiceless (vl), and word-final (wb) contexts

Table 7.18 Estimated marginal means (in Hz) for F_2 movement by environment and vowel for Midwestern White Speaker 13

Vowel	Context	Mean (Hz)	Std. error (Hz)	95% Confidence interval	
				Lower bound	Upper bound
/ɑ/	Voiced	3	48.331	−93	98
	Voiceless	−45	71.142	−186	96
/ai/	Voiced	−575	37.582	−650	−500
	Voiceless	−381	52.542	−485	−277

of vowel with context ($F(1,102) = 5.027$, $p < 0.027$). The estimated marginal means for the interaction (Table 7.18) shows that F_2 movement for /ɑ/ did not vary significantly by voicing context (a difference of 48 Hz), but did vary for /ai/ (a difference of 194 Hz). Speaker 13's F_2 movements for /ai/ (−575 Hz pre-voiced and −381 Hz pre-voiceless) are substantially greater than those of the AA group (−139 Hz pre-voiced and −164 Hz pre-voiceless) and the AP group (−214 Hz pre-voiced and −215 Hz pre-voiceless).

Table 7.19 Summary of /ai/ patterning by speaker. Differences in the third and fourth columns that are significant at the 0.05 level are in bold

Speaker	More movement for /ai/ than /ɑ/ in . . .	F_1/ai/ movement greater preceding . . .	F_2/ai/ movement greater preceding . . .
1	F_2	Voiceless	**Voiceless**
2	F_1 and F_2	**Voiceless**	Voiceless
3	F_2	Voiceless	Voiceless
4	F_1 and F_2	**Voiced**	Voiceless
5	F_1 and F_2	Voiced	Voiced
6	F_1 and F_2	**Voiced**	Voiceless
7	F_1 and F_2	**Voiced**	Voiceless
8	F_1 and F_2	**Voiced**	Voiced
9	F_1	Voiceless	Voiced
10	F_1 and F_2	Voiceless	Voiceless
11	n/a	Voiced	Voiceless
12	F_1 and F_2	**Voiced**	**Voiceless**
13	F_1 and F_2	**Voiced**	Voiced

7.2.4 Summary of speaker-by-speaker analysis

Table 7.19 summarizes the patterns for each speaker. The vowels of all speakers except 11 showed greater movement for /ai/ than /ɑ/ in at least one acoustic dimension, and most in both. Where voicing has a significant conditioning effect, the predominant pattern is for pre-voiced /ai/ to show greater movement than pre-voiceless possibly due to longer duration. This is in contrast with the traditional conditioning pattern of /ai/ glide-weakening in pre-voiced contexts and diphthongization in pre-voiceless contexts shown by the older AAs. Speaker 12 is exceptional in that voicing context had opposite effects on F_1 and F_2.

7.3 The patterning of /ai/ in Detroit African American English reported by Nguyen (2006)

Nguyen (2006) analyzed the patterning of /ai/ for both contemporary Detroit AAE data and a subset of Shuy, Wolfram, and Riley's Detroit AAE corpus collected in 1966. She used two methods for taking acoustic measurements of /ai/. One measure calculated the F_2 difference within the /ai/ diphthong between the nucleus (/a/) and the offlgide (/i). The second method examined the F_2 difference between the nucleus of the /ai/ diphthong and /ɪ/ (with /ɪ/ being extracted from tokens produced independently from the /ai/ diphthong, e.g. as in /bɪt/ "bit").

Major findings from Nguyen (2006) are broken down by following environment; she examined pre-voiced and pre-voiceless tokens. For pre-voiced tokens, males have more glide-reduction than females (94). Lower-status speakers show greater glide-reduction than higher-status speakers (96), and contemporary speakers show more glide-reduction than 1966 speakers (96).

For pre-voiceless environment, Nguyen (2006) analyzed both F_1 and F_2. In contrast to the results in my study, she found that contemporary speakers had no greater degree of glide-weakening in pre-voiceless environments than Wolfram's 1966 tokens (110). She analyzed this surprising finding, given my own (2003) findings, as a result of contrasting ideological stances concerning Detroit and the South between our two sets of speakers. I discuss these contrasting ideological stances further in Chapter 8.

7.4 Conclusion

In this chapter I have analyzed glide length of /ai/ and /ɑ/ by ethnicity, vowel, and context. Although there are many similarities in patterning between the AA and AP groups, there are several contrasts. In the group comparison that included the four youngest speakers of each ethnicity, the AP group has significantly greater /ai/ movement overall in the F_2 dimension. In the speaker-by-speaker analysis, I showed that the older AA speakers instantiate the traditional pattern of voicing conditioning on /ai/ by showing diphthongal pre-voiceless variants, in contrast to the younger AAs and the APs who show glide-weakening for the progressive pre-voiceless variant. The Detroit White woman showed greater movement for F_2 than either of the Southern migrant groups. The social salience of /ai/ will be discussed in Chapter 8. The finding that, as a group, younger AAs show pre-voiceless glide-weakening is an important one because the canonical pattern reported in the literature for AAE is for the /ai/ glide to be weakened in pre-voiced and word-final contexts but robust in pre-voiceless contexts. The results presented in this chapter add to the growing body of work (Mallinson *et al.* 2001; Anderson 2002, 2003; Anderson and Fridland 2002; Fridland 2004; Childs 2005) which suggests that pre-voiceless /ai/ glide-weakening is a change in progress for at least some speakers of AAE.

8

The Local and Supralocal Contexts for the Patterns of Usage

This chapter discusses and contextualizes the results for /u/ and /ʊ/ (Chapter 6) and /ai/ (Chapter 7) in terms of the local contact situation in Detroit as well as the supralocal context of American English. Section 8.1 provides comments on Detroit and its relationship to the suburbs. Participants discuss residential segregation, "White Flight" out of Detroit, perceptions concerning the suburbs, poverty and crime in Detroit, the 1967 riot, and Coleman Young, the first African American mayor of Detroit. Section 8.2 provides comments on migration, the South, and Southern cultural practices. Speakers discuss reverse migration and purchasing property in the South, ties to the South which include trips to South and loved ones who either remained in the South or returned there, rural cultural traditions brought to Detroit by first-generation migrants and persisting for later generations, relationships between African American and Appalachian White Southern migrants, the self-reported categories of "Southern" and "Hillbilly," and metapragmatic commentary on language.

8.1 Participant comments on Detroit and its relationship to the suburbs

In commenting on daily life, participants are offering interpretations on their conditions and situations and on everyday life in Detroit. Before each interview, the participants in this study were given a flyer that explained the purpose of the project.

We want to audiotape a series of conversations lasting between 45 and 60 minutes with Detroiters from a number of different neighborhoods. These will help us understand how developments over the last 40 years or so have affected men and women of different generations in their everyday lives. We will use the tapes to learn about changes in peoples' views of their work and their leisure and about the way Detroiters speak of their city and to each other. In short we want a record of what Detroiters' say about their city, at the beginning of the twenty first century. (Excerpt from the Flyer, Conversations in Motown at the turn of the century: Detroit people and Detroit neighborhoods, for The Detroit Project, Directed by Lesley Milroy at the University of Michigan)

/ai/ shows massive differentiation among socially salient groups in the Detroit area (Edwards 1997; Eckert 2000; Anderson 2003). Several themes emerge in the recorded interviews which provide a window into patterns of social indexing that are particularly helpful in understanding the patterning of /ai/ presented in Chapter 7. Section 8.1.1 provides comments from the interviews that reveal, for the African American participants, the salience of residential segregation, stances toward the suburbs, perceptions of the White exodus out of Detroit, the 1967 riot, Coleman Young, and the salience of poverty, lack of jobs, and other struggles that characterize life in the inner city. Section 8.1.2 presents commentary on migration, the South, differentiation between Southern migrants and Midwestern Whites, and Southern cultural practices as well as metapragmatic commentary on language.

8.1.1   Residential segregation

The sociologists Farley *et al.* describe Detroit as " . . . a metropolitan that is exceptionally segregated—by 1990, Detroit was more residentially segregated than other US metropolis" (2000: 161). Through extensive surveys of residents of Detroit and the suburbs of Detroit, these researchers compiled "residential isolation indexes" to measure the degree of segregation in the Detroit metro area. For Whites in the area, the index score was 92, which means " . . . that the typical White lived in a neighborhood where 92% of other residents were White" (163). Farley *et al.* conclude, "regardless of their poverty or prosperity, Detroit Whites generally lived in the suburbs and Blacks in the central city" (191), and that Detroit shows a "... long-run trend in racial isolation" (171).

In their interviews, African American participants frequently discussed racial segregation in the Detroit area.

(1) Detroit is a very, very prejudiced, segregated city. Most of the good jobs are in the suburbs because the Whites don't know when another riot might break out, and that keeps a lot of the minorities and poor White people from getting jobs because they don't have the cars to get out there. (Speaker 2, African American F, b. 1936)

(2) (Highs schools) are very segregated. The schools are still really fucked up. (Speaker 3, African American F, b. 1971)

My class was almost all Black. Out of about 600 students, 6 of them were White. (African American M, b. 1973, boyfriend of Speaker 3).

Comments (3) and (4) describe the composition of the neighborhoods in Detroit, mostly African American with some "poor Whites."

(3) Most of the neighborhoods are filled with Blacks and what some people refer to as poor Whites. I don't like to hear them referred to as that. (Speaker 2, African American F, b. 1936)

(4) Detroit is predominantly Black. (Speaker 5, African American F, b. 1974)

There is a perception shared by some of the participants that Detroit Whites live in the suburbs in order to minimize their contact with African Americans. In comment (5), Speaker 3 says, "Whites don't want to live here in the regular neighborhoods with us." Speaker 6, in comment (6) says, "Whites moved to the suburbs to get away from Black people."

(5) I don't know why Detroit remains to be so segregated. I guess it's because the Whites don't want to live here in the regular neighborhoods with us. But, you know, who gives a damn. If they don't like Detroit, to hell with them. (Speaker 3, African American F, b. 1971)

(6) Whites moved to the suburbs to get away from Black people. There is a dividing line between the city and the suburbs. Cross it, and its dangerous for a Black person to drive alone. . . . I hate having to live like that. (Speaker 6, African American F, b. 1967)

After the "White Flight" (described in Section 8.1.2), roads between the city and the suburbs served as a racial boundary. Before the mass exodus of Whites to the suburbs, Detroit enforced racial boundaries through zoning. It is interesting that residential racial boundaries persist in Detroit over space, time, and social upheavals such as the 1967 Riot (discussed in Section 8.1.5) as well as desegregation and the Civil Rights Movement.

(7) There was a lot of segregation in the South, but there was a lot of segregation in Detroit, too. We lived in zones. We lived in Zone 7; I'll never forget it, and the reason they had these zones was because there was designated schools for Blacks and designated schools for Whites . . . They didn't want Blacks to attend their schools. That's why we had zones, like you have zip codes now; we had zones, and we were designated to certain zones, and that's where we had to go. (Speaker 2, African American F, b. 1936)

Residential segregation is a fact of life in Detroit, as Farley *et al.* (2000) point out. The salience of residential segregation to the African American participants in this project is apparent in the excerpts from interviews above. Comment (6) above concisely describes the situation, "there is a dividing line between the city and the suburbs," and that dividing line is racial. In addition to discussing residential segregation, participants also discussed the "White Flight" from Detroit.

8.1.2 "White Flight" out of Detroit

In addition to racial segregation, Farley *et al.* (2000) also discuss the White exodus from Detroit at length in their extensive social science research project study of the Detroit metropolitan area. These researchers frame the exodus of White Detroiters to the suburbs as a way to create residential segregation based on race (2000: 146). One report estimates that Detroit has lost over 600,000 residents to the suburbs by the late 1980s (Widick 1989), and the trend continues

(Farley *et al.* 2000) Similar to the theme of residential segregation, African American participants also discussed the White exodus out of Detroit.

There is a perception among some participants that the "White Flight" is primarily a result of Whites fleeing the city after the infamous 1967 riot. However, there is also a perception that the "White Flight" is not just a historical event, but is an ongoing trend ("I even understand now that they're down at 22 mile," comment (1) below) with economic consequences ("A lot of people were out of a job because when the White people moved, they took their businesses with them," comment (2) below).

(1) The city was never the same again after that. After the riot they call it the "White Exodus." Most of the Whites left the city after that time. They went past 8 mile, 9 mile; I even understand now that they're down at 22 mile. Because this riot was with Blacks, the black population called it the "White Flight". That's what they call it. They all left the city. (Speaker 2, African American F, b. 1936)

(2) My mother told me Detroit was a whole lot better before the riots because of the "White Flight." ... A lot of people were out of a job because when the White people moved, they took their businesses with them. (Speaker 5, African American F, b. 1974)

Similar to the comments on residential segregation above in Section 8.1.1, there is the perception that the "White Flight" due to Whites wanting to minimize their contact with African Americans.

(3) The "White Flight" was due to Whites moving to the suburbs to get away from the Black people. (Speaker 6, African American F, b. 1967)

(5) Most White people left Detroit when the Blacks moved in. (Speaker 8, Appalachian White F, b. 1960)

(6) I'm going to tell you the truth. Detroit was very prejudiced. Whites moved out to the suburbs; we call it the "White Flight". (Speaker 1, African American F, b. 1927)

The next section discusses the relationship of Detroit and its suburbs, which also figured prominently in the participant interviews. The relationship between Detroit and its suburbs has also attracted attention from other scholars (Farley *et al.* 2000).

8.1.3 Suburbs

The patterns of residential segregation were so striking in the surveys conducted by Farley *et al.* (2000) that those researchers expanded the study: " . . . race is such a strong determinant of where one lives in metro Detroit that we explored the thinking behind neighborhood evaluations by using open-ended questions" on the topic of "desirability of the inner suburbs." The team of sociologists noted it was " . . . easy to summarize the explanations blacks gave for classifying the suburbs as undesirable: it is a racial issue" (Farley *et al.* 2000: 195). They summarize the results as follows:

> For African Americans, racial reasons overwhelm the other explanations for why suburbs are undesirable. And the finding that so many blacks reported specific incidents and went on at length . . . reveals that Detroit's blacks share a cognitive map of the suburban ring. It is one that sees most suburbs . . . as hostile to them. (196)

The participants in this study also commented on the social salience of Detroit's suburbs.

> (1) And they (people in the suburbs) feel like they can be that way cause they live out there, and they're rich. (Speaker 6, African American F, b. 1967)

Echoing what Farley *et al.* (2000: 195) describe as a Detroit African American "cognitive map" of a hostile suburban ring, Speaker 6 discusses racial profiling of African Americans by suburban police in comments (2) and (3).

> (2) There are places here in Michigan where I probably shouldn't drive alone . . . I guess that's just how people are. . . . Even some of the suburbs, you know, a dividing line, you're in Detroit and the next minute you're in a suburb, and they're like that, you know.

And you just have to be really careful, and I hate having to live like that. Well should I go here because I know how the police are here ... (Speaker 6, African American F, b. 1967)

(3) I didn't really hear my father talk about it (harassment of African Americans by police). I'm really starting to hear more about it now that I'm older and on my own. I guess because they're getting more outlandish with it. They're going to pull somebody over because (pause). But when I was growing up I didn't hear that much about it like I do now. You know, it's almost an everyday thing. Well, I won't say every day, but it happens more often than not. And those are close suburbs, not way out in the upper part of Michigan but in the surrounding Detroit suburbs. And I think that's really bad. I really do because there are Black people that live in the suburbs. So, what do they do? They get pulled over. Yeah, if you get pulled over ... There was this one case where the mayor, Mayor Archer's son was pulled over in the suburb, Royal Oak, if I'm not mistaken. He was pulled over because they said he fit a description of a bank robber, but I mean if you're not doing over the speed limit or whatever, there's no reason for him to be handcuffed and thrown in the back of the police car, so you know, as they say it is the nineties, and that stuff still happening. So, I'm surprised at it being the nineties and we still have to go through stuff like that, that blatant out of order behavior from people. Where were they raised? In Michigan. They're a cop. Or they had to have lived in ... Detroit or the surrounding areas. Where were they raised where they were taught this way? (Speaker 6, African American F, b. 1967)

Farley *et al.* suggest, " ... less obvious forms of discrimination continue to maintain Detroit as one of the most segregated places in the nation, ... including the tendency of some suburban police officers to stop young male drivers who are Black more frequently than those who are White" (2000: 264).

Not only did Whites abandon Detroit for the suburbs, so did corporations and businesses. Widick (1989: xiv) argues that " ... a powerful force ... which negatively affects Detroit ... is the impact of the decisions of the power structure—the auto industry leaders, the big merchandisers, and the ... investors—to shift the bulk of its plants, stores, investments, and activities outside the city." Participant comments (4) and (5) explicitly link "White Flight" with a loss of good jobs in Detroit.

(4) We don't need ya'll people and businesses in the suburbs. We don't need this, and we don't need that, but we did, and that's how everything got so bad.... (Speaker 5, African American F, b. 1974)

(5) Most of the good jobs are in the suburbs because the Whites don't know when another riot might break out, and that keeps a lot of the minorities and the poor people from getting jobs because they don't have the cars to get out there. (Speaker 2, African American F, b. 1936)

Once again, as in the previous sections of this chapter, a perception that Whites moved to the suburbs to distance themselves from the African American population of Detroit is described in comment (6).

(6) Mostly they (Whites) move out to the suburbs to get away from Black people, but not all Black people are like that. I've worked, well, since 18. (Speaker 6, African American F, b. 1967)

The social salience of racial segregation dividing the city from the suburbs is apparent in comment (7).

(7) They (African Americans in the city) hate them, the White people in the suburbs, but oh well. (Speaker 5, African American F, b. 1974)

The contrast in the material conditions of the suburbs versus the city is also socially salient. Residing in the suburbs means having access to a better education, better roads, better jobs, and better opportunities.

(8) My friend Tiffany grew up in West Bloomfield, and I used to wonder what it would be like to go to an all-White school. (Speaker 5, African American F, b. 1974)

Comment (9) is especially interesting because it highlights social differentiation between Whites who stayed in Detroit and those who live in the suburbs.

(9) We are different than "suburbanites". Most White people left Detroit when the Blacks moved in. Our apartment on the Northeast side of Detroit was $235 a month. It wasn't safe. (Speaker 8, Appalachian White F, b. 1960)

Suburbanites would have been able to live there. They would have been killed. (Detroit White M, husband of Speaker 8)

Speaker 8, as well as her husband, calls residents of the suburbs "suburbanites" and explicitly points out how they, as city dwellers, are different from "suburbanites." Speaker 8 describes herself as having grown up in a "regular neighborhood" in Detroit and discusses how her parents would not leave Detroit during the "White Flight." She discusses how her parents were well integrated into their neighborhood and how she and her husband also chose to live in Detroit.

Chapter 3 discussed the demographic differences between the inner city as well as the inner and outer suburbs of Detroit. The outer suburbs are affluent; the inner suburbs are more stable than the inner city, and the urban center has a poverty level of over 50% (SEMCOG 1994). In other words, there is a continuum of affluence in the Detroit metropolitan region with the outer suburbs and inner city constituting the two extremes.

A report on community leadership for the twenty-first century, based on results from an 18-month project that generated detailed case studies of 10 major metropolitan regions (including Detroit), also discusses the disparities between the inner cities and the suburbs in terms of crossing a line, similar to the way Speaker 6 described the dividing line between the city and the suburbs in comment (3).

It is impossible not to notice the dramatic differences in economic prosperity within the region. Crossing the street from East Detroit to Grosse Pointe Park is like moving from a underdeveloped country into an enclave of the wealthy. Nowhere else in the United States is the line between the haves and the have-nots as clear or as abrupt. . . . The Detroit metropolitan area has as far to go as any other region in the country in dealing with both racial and socioeconomic segregation. (Parr 1998, accessed via the internet at http://www.academy.umd.edu/Publications/boundary/Case Studies/csdetroit.htm)

In the course of fieldwork, I drove through the area described above: East Detroit to Grosse Pointe Park, where I conducted an interview with a wealthy resident of that suburb. Literally, a single road divides poverty-stricken East Detroit from the luxury homes of Grosse Pointe Park. Section 8.1.4 discusses the poverty and crime facing Detroit.

8.1.4 Poverty, scarcity of jobs, and crime in Detroit

Participants also discussed poverty, difficulty in finding employment, and crime in Detroit. In fact, Detroit has a national reputation as a city in crisis:

> Or consider the Detroit region. It reluctantly serves as the stereotype of a region in chronic crisis. Nearly every adversity that could befall a major city happened there—from the competitive meltdown of its jewel, the American automobile industry, to urban flight that created the most hollowed out core of all American cities, leaving in its wake hundreds of acres of urban wasteland. For years in the 1980s and early-90s, Detroit failed to register a single housing start. (Peirce and Johnson 1998, accessed via the internet at http://www.academy. umd.edu/Publications/boundary/CaseStudies/bcsdetroit.htm)

The participants discussed how difficult life is in Detroit, particularly for residents of the inner city.

> (1) Life is hard on Black people in the city, especially in Detroit. It's sad because nobody cares how folks are living here. (Speaker 5, African American F, b. 1974)

> (2) It wasn't very easy to get a job in Detroit. (Speaker 8, Appalachian White F, b. 1960)

Speaker 1 discusses how she and her family lacked enough food while her husband was looking for work.

(3) There have been days I didn't have the money to buy it (food), and a lot of nights I would go to bed hungry cause I would feed the kids before I would eat. Um hm. And when I was down South, I never did go hungry. I always had food. It might not have been the best of food, but it was food. Then when I come here, married, kids, go to bed hungry at night. I just couldn't believe that. I just couldn't believe that. I really couldn't. I didn't know it until then because I used to cry myself to sleep. (Speaker 1, African American F, b. 1927)

Speaker 2 described the decline of Detroit, beginning after the 1967 riot.

(4) You could see a decline. Going down, going down. (Speaker 2, African American F, b. 1936)

Speaker 8 and her husband, who are both White, describe gun fire in their neighborhood as "not a big deal to us." The landlord they rented from gave them a reduced rent to serve as security for the business downstairs from their apartment.

(5) We had guests one evening for dinner, and walked them out to their car and heard gun fire right up the street. Not a big deal to us, but they were walking fast to their car. . . . That was very, very common. (Speaker 8, Appalachian White F, b. 1960)

The reason the guy who owned the business let us live there is to keep an eye on the building, so in a sense we were security. (Detroit White M, husband of Speaker 8)

There was a guy across the street who sold drugs. (Speaker 8, Appalachian White F, b. 1960)

Speaker 8's husband comments at length on the ineffectiveness of Detroit's police.

(5 continued) . . . call the police and nobody comes. And an hour later, and there's nobody there. They are fucking lying. There is no police response times. There is no police response time. (Detroit White M, husband of Speaker 8)

Hanging out the party store or hanging out at the whore house. (Speaker 8, Appalachian White F, b. 1960)

The disintegration of Detroit . . . Big out-of-control organizations that are falling apart. I was never much impressed by what I saw. An old good-old-boy network of White boys. They were indolent, and didn't do much. . . . report takers at best. And it was never ending. (Detroit White M, husband of Speaker 8)

I remember trick-or-treating on Jefferson, and a man came out of Burger King chasing someone with a baseball bat. 380 fires on Devil's Night one night. So many abandoned houses. . . . You asked "is it getting better?" No . . . It really is not a real city. It really is not a real city. (Speaker 8, Appalachian White F, b. 1960)

The city is depopulated. Many less people live there than in my youth. Worthless police officers, fat ass White police officers. (Detroit White M, husband of Speaker 8)

The characterization of Detroit police officers as "a good-old boy network of White boys" and "worthless . . . fat ass White police officers" by Speaker 8's husband is particularly interesting because he is also White, but he clearly differentiates himself from White police officers.

As Speaker 8 pointed out in comment (2), the employment situation in Detroit is grim and life in the inner city is difficult. A government report issued in March 2007 listed Detroit as having the highest rate for job loss in the nation for last year for a metropolitan area (http://www.bls.gov/news.release/metro.nr0.htm). In addition to the difficulties in securing employment in Detroit, this section also discussed crime and poverty in the inner city. Section 8.1.5 describes the 1967 riot, a key historical moment in Detroit.

8.1.5 Riots

The 1967 riot in Detroit has been described as the worst race riot in U.S. history:

In 1967, the city suffered the most agonizing race riot in U.S. history. It began with a police raid on an after-hours drinking spot, and ended with forty-three killed, 7,000 arrested, and damage of more than $30 million. One result was more white flight and a majority African-American city. (Parr 1998, accessed through the internet at http://www.academy. umd.edu/Publications/boundary/CaseStudies/bcsdetroit.htm)

The riot was discussed not only by older participants, who experienced it, but also by younger participants.

(1) Detroit has never been the same since the 1967 riot because they tore the city up. They set things a-fire, looted stores, and did everything they thought they could get away with. But prior to that, there wasn't a nicer place to live than the city of Detroit, MI.... We went back down after the riot and it was just like a war zone, piles of ashes still smoldering and smoking, and they had cut off the expressway. Couldn't get in and couldn't out. After a week went by we could get in. (Speaker 2, African American F, b. 1936)

(2) The National Guard was worse than the people that were fighting. They did so wrong. They did really wrong. Ummhmm. In the 1967 riot they didn't get away with it... Because people was killing the Guard. (Speaker 1, African American F, b. 1927)

(3) The factory shut down during the 67 riot. We got off early that day. (Speaker 7, Appalachian White F, b. 1931)

(4) And I know my mother told me the reason why Detroit is like it is 1) the riot and 2) after the riots Coleman Young took office and it really just got bad. (Speaker 5, African American F, b. 1974)

The riot forever changed Detroit, as noted by Speaker 2 in comment (1), "Detroit has never been the same since the 1967 riot." Speaker 1, in comment (2), comments on the force used by the National Guard to stop the riot: "The National Guard was worse than the people that were fighting. They did so wrong. They did really wrong." Widick (1989: 186) describes the aftermath of the 1967 riot as "... a backlash of Black rage and White fear, the extent of which was seldom comprehended." Speaker 5's comment (4) is especially noteworthy because of the report that her mother reasons "Detroit is like it is" due, in part, to the riot and also to the leadership of Coleman Young. The stance that Coleman Young contributed to the decline of Detroit was not shared by any of the other participants in this study. The older African American participants (Speaker 1 and Speaker 2), in particular, described the leadership of Coleman Young as bright spot in the history of Detroit.

8.1.6 Coleman Young, first African American Mayor of Detroit

Coleman Young was frequently mentioned in the interviews. Young was a first-generation Southern migrant who was born in Alabama. He was the first African American mayor of Detroit and served five consecutive terms as Mayor of Detroit, easily winning each election. Detroit underwent massive transformation during Young's tenure:

> African-American Mayor Coleman Young, who took office in 1973, took a blunt, pragmatic approach to Detroit's realities. In 1977, the city's $350 million Renaissance Center opened with skyscraping office and hotel towers. The massive development led to more than $600 million in other downtown investment. The auto industry reinvested in Detroit, as well.

> But the problems in the 1970s continued.... Whites fled, with population declining by more than 300,000 people. The city found itself stuck with city wages well above those of comparable cities, and in 1981, bankruptcy looked like the next step. Once again, the city rallied. Young trimmed more than 4,000 from city staff, coaxed residents into supporting a doubling of city taxes, and convinced those still on the city payroll to take major pay cuts. (Young)... pulled (Detroit) back from the brink of disaster. (Parr 1998, accessed through the internet at http://www. academy.umd.edu/Publications/boundary/CaseStudies/bcsdetroit. htm)

Speaker 2, in particular, echoes Parr's comment that "(Young)... pulled (Detroit) back from the brink of disaster": *(Young) brought the city to where it was, but now I see it on a decline.... Coleman Young brought the city back from the 67 riot.*

(1) They're on the mend. They're trying to bring the city back, but as far as I'm concerned it will never be the same. It will never be the same. And their choice to bring the gambling casinos down there, I think that's the worst decision the city could have ever made. The last mayor that died last year, was the mayor Coleman Young, he brought the city to where it was, but now I see it on a decline.

Coleman Young brought the city back from the 67 riot, and the first thing he did when he got into office. I do believe that was the first black mayor of the city of Detroit.

Speaker 2 also points out the Coleman Young ended institutionalized racial profiling by the Detroit police force.

They had a program called Stress. They used to stop young black men on the street because they were afraid of them, and search them, check for weapons, so when Coleman Young got into office, he said "no we're going to stop this. This is discrimination. If you're going to stop the young black men, you're going to stop all of them." So he took that out.

Coleman Young had a reputation of "fighting for the seniors" (see below), one manifestation of which was instituting a free bus ride program for senior citizens.

And then he started to bring in all kinds of different stuff. He wanted free (bus) rides for the seniors... He fought a lot for the seniors, and when Coleman Young died this is one person that cried. I really cried when he died. He had free ride for the seniors...

Young also had a reputation for using profanity. Speaker 2 also reports that "he gave a lot jobs to minorities... that never had good jobs before."

My brother asked why Coleman Young used all that profanity. I told my brother because that is all some people understand. He gave jobs to a lot of minorities, not only blacks, minorities... that had never had good jobs before. You don't remember and your parents don't, but the only jobs they would give Blacks was the dirtiest and lowest jobs. You probably don't remember, even your parents don't remember, but the only jobs they would give to blacks was cleaning, the dirtiest and lowest paying jobs they could find. That's why my dad had to work two jobs because, having a large family, one check was not enough, so that was why he had to work two jobs. (Speaker 2, African American F, b. 1936)

Speaker 1 and her husband also commented on Coleman Young.

(2) Coleman did a lot for the seniors. The man was in office five terms. He got free (bus) rides for the seniors. (African American M, husband of Speaker 1)

The only thing I didn't like about Coleman was that he cussed so much. He cussed on the news, and little children be watching the news. (Speaker 1, African American F, b. 1927)

The only Appalachian White participant who lived in the city instead of the inner suburbs also comments favorably on Young.

(3) I liked Coleman Young. My parents are pretty down about Archer (the mayor of Detroit at the time of the interview). Archer is trying to throw my parents out of their house, condemn it and give them $30,000. (Speaker 8, Appalachian White F, b. 1960)

Coleman Young is an important figure in the social landscape of Detroit for city residents. Note that the only Appalachian speaker to actually reside in the city instead of in a suburb is Speaker 8, the only Appalachian participant to comment on Young. This same participant was also the only Appalachian participant to comment on crime and lack of jobs in Detroit in Section 8.1.4.

8.2 Participant comments on migration, the South, and Southern cultural practices

For both the African American and Appalachian White participants, general cultural orientation to the South emerged during the fieldwork phase of the study. This section discusses the plans of some of the participants to return to the South, ties to the South, aspects of Southern culture described by participants, comments by African American participants about Appalachian White Southern migrants as well as comments by Appalachian Southern migrants concerning African American Southern migrants, and explicit commentary on language.

Participants reported where they or their families migrated from in the South, which is discussed in Section 8.2.1.

8.2.1   Reverse migration and purchasing property in the South

(1) I am from Waycross, Georgia. Do you know where that is? (Speaker 1, African American F, b. 1927)

(2) My mom was from West Virginia; my father was from Alabama. (Speaker 2, African American F, b. 1936)

(3) My grandparents came to Detroit from Georgia. My grandpa wanted to make a better life. (Speaker 3, African American F, b. 1971)

(4) My family is from the Carolinas. (Speaker 4, African American F, b. 1974)

(5) My parents are from Greeneville, South Carolina. (Speaker 6, African American F, b.1967)

(6) I'm from Ranger, North Carolina. A lot of Southern people came from the Carolinas and Tennessee. We lived on Tennessee Street. There's been people from the South coming up here ever since then. (Speaker 7, Appalachian White F, b. 1931)

(7) My parents eloped in 1954, went to Georgia, got married, and then they moved here. A lot of Southerners migrated, lots of jobs. There was job availability here. (Speaker 8, Appalachian White F, b. 1960)

(8) My mom is from Murphy, North Carolina. (Speaker 9, Appalachian White F, b. 1951)

(9) My grandfather came to Detroit in the early twenties to work in the auto factories, and many people from Franklin did. He didn't stay long, was a carpenter, found work and moved back to

Franklin. My grandmother was dying of cancer, and she wanted to go home to die. My parents moved to Detroit after they grew up. My grandfather's brother and kids also moved up. The only family we ever had here was Uncle Frank's family. Grandpa and Grandma moved back to Franklin and bought 118 acres. (Speaker 10, Appalachian White F, b. 1949)

(10) We are both from Nantahala, North Carolina, in Macon County. (Speaker 11, Appalachian White F, b. 1936)

(11) We are from Hiawassee Dam (in North Carolina). (Speaker 12, Appalachian White F, b. 1965)

Berry (2000) discusses The Great Southern Migration as being kin-based, and a few participants in my study also discussed migration in those terms.

(12) I have a brother and sister in Detroit. It wasn't too bad for me, after I got used to it, because I had relatives up here. And they all stayed. We have a big family. Half of them are up here, half in North Carolina. (Speaker 11, Appalachian White F, b. 1936)

(13) I had two brothers here ahead of me. Another brother came up at the same time; the four of us in a car going up, 18 hours. My two other brothers were in Hamtramck. We lived in a duplex with six family members. There was a lot of Southern people there. My nephew came up to work and people I knew from all around there. (Speaker 7, Appalachian White F, b. 1931)

Bridget: Well that probably helped

Oh yeah and we'd go visit them and they'd come visit us. Yeah that did help. (Speaker 7, Appalachian White F, b. 1931)

Several participants discussed their plans to move back to the South, and some already had property there. Reverse migration for Southern migrants is not unique to Southern migrants in Detroit. It is reported for Southern migrants in other regions of the Midwest by Berry (2000) and in California (Gregory 2005)

Speaker 5 contrasts the reports about the South from Detroit friends who are moved back down South with conditions in inner city

Detroit. She described her goal as "getting out of Detroit and going South."

(14) I have friends in . . . Atlanta, some of the other Southern states. And they're from here, they come back after going to these Southern places and talk about how much better it is for people—no matter what color you are. My mother was about to move to Atlanta. I was going to go to Emery University. We were out of here, but my grandmother took ill. This was right before she passed, so we ended up staying. But most of the people we grew up with, they moved (South) at some point, so it's like we the only people still here! Why? Why are we still here? So I made it my goal that when I graduate and find myself doing whatever it is I call myself doing , I'm outta here. I hate Detroit. I don't care if I'm fifty, I'm getting out of Detroit and going South. I hate it. I really do. (Speaker 5, African American F, b. 1974)

Not only does Speaker 12 plan on moving back down South, she and her husband already own property in North Carolina and spend "at least a month every summer" there. Like Speaker 5 above, Speaker 12 indicates that moving back South is a goal: "We've always tried to get back South."

(15) I'm counting the days until my husband retires from Ford so we can move back South. I always have a fabulous phone bill from calling down South. I keep close contact with my family. We bought a place in the South. My parents live there now. That's the only place we vacation at. That's where we go every summer. We go at least three times a year. I would stay down there at least a month every summer. Last summer my dad died. I was practically there all summer. We usually go at the end of May. (Speaker 12, Appalachian White F, b. 1965)

She has more friends down there than she does here. (Appalachian M, husband of Speaker 12)

We've always tried to get back South. One Yankee woman once said, "Maybe they'll move back South". Give us a break, people. We already have our home (back South). When we retire

South . . . maybe we can take some real vacations because from up here we've always gone to North Carolina, 99% of the time. (Speaker 12, Appalachian White F, b. 1965)

Speakers 7 and 10 also own property in the South.

(16) I have a trailer down South. (Speaker 7, Appalachian White F, b. 1931)

(17) I bought a house in Franklin. I spent winters in Michigan and summers in North Carolina without my husband. He's not very fond of the South and will never live there. My husband said, "You don't need a house down there." "Yes I do," I said, "The door is closing on my life down there, and it's only open a crack." (Speaker 10, Appalachian White F, b. 1949)

Speaker 9 commented on the reverse migration of some of her husband's African American coworkers.

(18) My husband works with a lot of African Americans at Chrysler. Most of them have homes built down there, no plans of staying up here after they retire. Most of them are going back (South). (Speaker 9, Appalachian White F, b. 1951)

She also indicated the she and her husband hope to purchase property down South:

(19) We really like it down South . . . .We are really thinking about getting a place down there. That's what we're hoping to do when he retires. (Speaker 9, Appalachian White F, b. 1951)

This section discussed the migration history of each of the participants as well as comments by some of the participants that they either plan to move back down South (reverse migration) or, in some cases, already own property in the South. The next section discusses participant comments regarding ties to the South, including trips and visits back South and relatives still residing in the South.

8.2.2   Ties to the South: Trips and relatives

Regular and repeated trips from Detroit to the South were frequently mentioned in the interviews. A few participants even reported periodically moving back down South, particularly when the employment situation in Detroit faltered.

(1) My father's family moved back and forth constantly. He would spend maybe two weeks here and then go back South. (Speaker 8, Appalachian White F, b. 1960)

(2) My brothers, every time they'd get laid off they'd take off back down South. Every time he'd (her husband) get a long weekend, we'd take off and go. (Speaker 7, Appalachian White F, b. 1931)

Bridget: That's a long drive just for a long weekend.

I know, but you'd get so homesick, not just for the people but also for the mountains, too. There's none around here, you know. Wall to wall people and all that. Concrete and everything, you know. It was hard on us. In 1957 my husband was laid off for three years, and we moved back down South lock, stock and barrel, took everything. We came back to Detroit in 1961. You had to come up here to make a living cause there was no way down there. I used to go down there and stay for months at a time. (Speaker 7, Appalachian White F, b. 1931)

Speaker 1 sent her children down South for several months once when times were particularly difficult.

(3) After the war, a lot of people lost their jobs. We liketa starved to death. My mother had the kids down South. I didn't want them to go hungry. (Speaker 1, African American F, b. 1927)

In addition to the excerpts from participant interviews above, in which a few participants described owning property in the South, Speakers 12 and 10 described extended visits to the South during the summer months. Speaker 12's 13-year-old daughter spends every single summer in the Southern Appalachian mountains with her grandparents.

(4) My husband and I go back and forth South, staying at least a month most every summer. My daughter always spends the summer in North Carolina [she was in North Carolina at the time of the interview]. I don't think she has ever spent a summer in Michigan. The mountains are always home. The longer we live up here I think "well, its not so bad", but when we're driving home and I'm looking at the Tellico Mountains I think "oh, this is what I do love". (Speaker 12, Appalachian White F, b. 1965)

Speaker 10 ran away from home (in Detroit) at age 11 and spent the next 6 years in Franklin, North Carolina with her grandparents.

(5) As a small child, we got in a car, I'm one of three girls, and we'd go spend two weeks with grandfather (in Franklin, North Carolina). My father kept making trips down. As a small child, we'd go spend two or three weeks with Grandpa, with the animals, and it was magic. I loved it. We visited old people with Grandfather. So, we'd spend the summer there until I was eleven. I hitchhiked down South to grandpa's when I was eleven. A man driving an eighteen wheeler truck drove me all the way to grandpa's. I stayed there six years. It was magic growing up. I got summer jobs . . . We didn't have much. I worked for an uncle farming and learned a lot on the farm. Finally it was the end of my junior year, my grandfather said I needed to go back North. I had a boyfriend, etc. I wasn't interested in leaving. I still spend every summer on the mountain in Franklin. The ones I knew that are the most important to me are going to be gone. There isn't anyone on the mountain that doesn't know me. Everyone knows me and I know everyone. It is like time stopped and I can go back and still get the magic. It is still magic to me. Still see my aunt quite often. (Speaker 10, Appalachian White F, b. 1949)

One factor that contributes to a sense of a Southern "homeland" is that the participants, even second- and third-generation migrants, still maintain contact with family that either remained in or returned to the South.

(6) When I was growing up, my parents still went down South to family reunions. (Speaker 6, African American F, b. 1967)

(7) I've got family still down there; that's the thing. (Speaker 12, Appalachian White F, b. 1965)

(8) I miss family most of all. That was the hardest thing about coming up here—leaving your family. I'd get so homesick I'd just sit and cry. I wrote them letters. I couldn't call; they didn't have no phones then.... That was what was so hard to do; when we first come up here was leaving the family behind like that. (Speaker 7, Appalachian White F, b. 1931)

The excepts from the interviews in this section make it clear that both the African American and Appalachian White Southern migrants continue to maintain ties to the South, evident in visits to the South and family ties still in the South. The next section discusses Southern cultural practices maintained by the Southern migrants.

8.2.3 Southern cultural practices in Detroit

Participant interviews revealed that they maintain a variety of Southern cultural practices, including food, burial practices, religious traditions such as church homecomings, caring for the sick and elderly, and researching family genealogy.

Comment (1) indexes a differentiation in the identification of "place of origin" between Southerners and non-Southerners. A stereotypical characteristic of the South is that you cannot be "from" a particular place unless your family goes back several generations in the area. Indeed, I myself was raised with that understanding.

(1) When somebody asks us where we're from, we say we're from Hiwassee Dam, North Carolina. If you ask an outsider where they are from, it's the latest place they've lived. (Speaker 12, Appalachian White F, b. 1965)

Comment (2) describes how Southerners still raise their gardens in Detroit.

(2) A lot of people got they garden, like we got a garden here. Before we had a garden, I was looking at the neighbor's garden. His wife asked, "Are you from down South?" I said "Yes I am." She

said, "You want some of these vegetables don't you?" I said, "um hum." She give me greens, she give me okra; she gave me corn; she gave me tomatoes. She just fixed up a basket and gave it to me. (Speaker 1, African American F, b. 1927)

Speaker 1 also describes how she arranged to have grits, a Southern staple, imported to Detroit from the South before the time that Detroit merchants began to carry them in their stores.

(3) I love grits. I love grits. (Her husband stated that there were no grits in Detroit when they first moved up from Georgia). So, I go to the store, and I say "you got any grits?" "What is that?" I said "grits", and I couldn't tell them what it was. All I knew was grits. I didn't even know what grits was made of. I think I started Detroit having grits cause I asked for them so much. I wrote my daddy. I told him to send me some grits because they didn't have grits here, and he sent me a five pound bag of grits, and I went and showed it to the man at the store. (Speaker 1, African American F, b. 1927)

Speaker 9 taught the cook at a Warren (inner suburb of Detroit) restaurant to make Southern breakfast gravy because they brought her unacceptable, non-breakfast (i.e. non-sausage) gravy when she ordered gravy with her breakfast. Notice how Speaker 9 told the wait-person "I am from the South," even though she is a second-generation migrant.

(4) We went out to breakfast once and I ordered gravy. They brought me chicken gravy. I said, "Excuse me this is not breakfast gravy." They said it was. I said, "Well, I'm from the South and this is not it. I tell you what, you take me back to your kitchen and I'll show you how to make Southern breakfast gravy." And I did. I made them a pot of (sausage) gravy. My granny taught me how to make it. (Speaker 9, Appalachian White F, b. 1951)

This speaker also cooks Southern food for her family, and her grand-daughter's favorite food is fried okra, a Southern delicacy.

(5) My granddaughter's favorite food is fried okra. (Speaker 9, Appalachian White F, b. 1951)

Like Speaker 9 above, Speaker 4—an African American—identifies herself as Southern: "A lot of people from the South are up here, and we barbeque on our front porches." Speaker 4 is third generation.

(6) Detroit is a mixture between the North and the South: the hospitality of the South plus the big city life of the North. A lot of people from the South are up here, and we barbeque on our front porches. One way you know a Southern person in Detroit is when you go over to their house for the first time and get a huge dinner. (Speaker 4, African American F, b. 1974)

Burial practices are another important cultural tradition. The daughter of Speaker 7 died as a young adult, and Speaker 7 took her back to the family graveyard for burial instead of burying her in Michigan, where her daughter had lived her entire life.

(7) All my people are going to be buried in the family graveyard in North Carolina. Even though I raised my daughter in Michigan I took her back to the family graveyard to be buried. (Speaker 7, Appalachian White F, b. 1927)

Speaker 10 has already purchased her plot in the "family row" back at her family's church in North Carolina. In fact, although she is a third-generation migrant, she is a member of that church since she is able to attend regularly during the summer (see Section 8.2.2).

(8) I'm going to be buried in my family row (back down South). I've got it all taken care of, and I know where I'm going to go. I'm going to be there with my people. My uncle said, "You're going to be buried at your home church." So he took me up to my family church (in Franklin, North Carolina), of which I am a member, and he showed me my family row. They were worried somebody would take my spot. So, I had to put a footstone with my initials, and I feel good about that. So I've got it all taken care of. I'm going be there with my people. My husband is going to be

cremated. That's my story. You have any questions? (Speaker 10, Appalachian White F, b. 1949)

(9) Being Southern, when someone dies, we take food to the family's house. (Speaker 7, Appalachian White F, b. 1927)

Speaker 8 reports that Detroit used to have a festival for Southern migrants, and Speaker 9 describes many kinds of cultural events and get-togethers for Southerners.

(10) Detroit used to have "The Southern Festival". (Speaker 8, Appalachian White F, b. 1960)

(11) There were picnics out on (Highway) 94 for people from Kentucky, plus Freedom Hill. There's several different places that have bluegrass (music). There's a lot of stuff going on up here for Southern people. Got to keep your roots. There's quite a few things that go on that are strictly Southern based. Potlucks. (Speaker 9, Appalachian White F, b. 1951)

Speaker 8 also described parties in her childhood neighborhood, an inner city Southern migrant enclave.

(12) (Inner City Southern Appalachian) people would have like these he haw parties every week, and that's just what you do. You drink whisky and pull out your gun and shoot out the street lights things like that. (Speaker 8, Appalachian White F, b. 1960)

The cultural anthropologist Hartigan (1999) also described these sorts of parties in Corktown, an Appalachian enclave in Southwestern Detroit.

(13) Something else that should be here (in Michigan) is homecoming. I wish we had that here, makes people closer as a congregation. I wish they had that here, picnic on the cemetery grounds. I am a member of a church down there (in the South). I go to homecoming, was baptized down there. (Speaker 10, Appalachian White F, b. 1949)

Speaker 10, who revealed in comment (5) of Section 8.2.2 that she ran away from home in Detroit to live with her grandfather down South at age 11, maintains close friendships with her girlfriends down South.

> (14) My girlfriends sent me a tee-shirt that says GRITS—girls raised in the South. Floats real well around town. (Speaker 10, Appalachian White F, b. 1949)

Speaker 10 is also the family historian and the "keeper of the family pictures."

> (15) I do the family genealogy. I have over 300 pictures. I am the keeper of the family pictures. I have the family history. (Speaker 10, Appalachian White F, b. 1949)

Other important cultural Southern traditions include dropping everything to be with loved ones in the event of a death in the family, and family members being present in around-the-clock shifts when loved ones are hospitalized. Having myself grown up in the rural Smoky Mountains of Western North Carolina, I understand that there is literally nothing—not school, employment, or anything else—that takes priority over family during these times.

> (16) If someone dies, I'll drive all night to be there for the family. There, if somebody's in the hospital, you stay by their side all night. You don't leave your loved one and go home. You stay there in the chair and you sleep. (Speaker 10, Appalachian White F, b. 1949)
>
> Bridget: Somebody's there all the time.
>
> And when they get bad in the nursing home, it's the same thing. I take my shift. (Speaker 10, Appalachian White F, b. 1949)

This section described the maintenance of Southern cultural practices by the African American and Appalachian White Southern migrant participants, such as strong kinship ties, burial practices, food, and gardening. The next section discusses comments made by participants on the relationship between Southern Whites and Southern African Americans in the Detroit area.

8.2.4 Relationship between Southern Whites and Southern African Americans

This section presents participant comments centering on the topic of relations between Southern Whites and Southern African Americans in Detroit.

Comments (1) and (2) describe neighborhoods as "mostly Black" with some White Southerners.

> (1) Some White Southerners live in the city, but most White people live in the suburbs, and Detroit is mostly Black. (Speaker 3, African American F, b. 1971)

> (2) I lived in an integrated neighborhood growing up. Most of the neighborhoods are filled with Blacks and what some people refer to as "poor Whites", which I don't agree with that term, but that's the term that they use. Most of them are from the South, and I don't think they should be called "poor White". (Speaker 2, African American F, b. 1936)

Speaker 7, a retired factory worker, reports that African American and White Southern migrants worked together in the factories.

> (3) Black and White Southerners worked together (in the factories), carpooled together, and got along very good. (Speaker 7, Appalachian White F, b. 1927)

Speaker 9 describes one cultural similarity between African American and White Southern migrants as being the preparation of Southern food.

> (4) There's a lot of similarities between Black and White Southern people. For one thing, we like to cook and eat Southern food. I don't have a racist bone in my body. I don't look at a person for their color. My husband doesn't like store bought food or restaurant stuff. I cook all the time and the guys at work say, "Ali,

you married to a Black woman." He says, "No I'm not." They say, "Yes you are. White women don't cook like that." He'd have pork chops smothered in onion gravy, corn. The correlation between African American and Southern White people is ... if you're from the South, you cook. You can't tell the difference. My husband would have pork chops smothered in onion gravy. And for breakfast he loves .... you know, sausage gravy. (Speaker 9, Appalachian White F, b. 1951)

Speaker 8 discusses the problems with bussing, in an integration attempt, when she attended school: "The students never got along, especially White students who grew up in neighborhoods without Black people." Recall that Speaker 8 is the only Appalachian White participant whose family remained in the inner city, and once again she contrasts herself with other Whites who live in neighborhoods without African American residents: "Of course, I grew up with Black people, and I always got along with everyone."

(5) I had a very poor education. Classes were way overcrowded ... very poor.... Poor education. The city started bussing ... trying to integrate the schools. Lots of little riots every single day. The students never got along, especially White students who grew up in neighborhoods without Black people. Of course, I grew up with Black people, and I always got along with everyone. (Speaker 8, Appalachian White F, b. 1960)

Although Speaker 12 and her husband resided in the suburbs at the time of the interview, they recalled growing up in the city and commented on similarities and differences in treatment of African American and Appalachian White Southern migrants by non-Southern Detroit Whites.

(6) Southern Whites in the inner city. It was because they didn't have a lot of money. (Appalachian White M, husband of Speaker 12)

A lot of things they (African Americans) went through was because they were poor and poor (White) people suffer the same thing. When I grew up, we still had an outhouse, no inside running water until sixth grade. The Northerners treated the Blacks worse than the (White) Southerners. When I was working, I thought they (society) think we're prejudiced because we're from the South. But... I remember when I was working... it was during the time economics was bad everywhere... My boss said, "Why don't they hassle the hillbillies?" (Speaker 12, Appalachian White F, b. 1965)

I had African American kids as friends, and my dad wouldn't support residential segregation. The neighborhood wanted to buy a house to keep Blacks out. My family would not support that. (Appalachian White M, husband of Speaker 12)

Speaker 12 also comments on cultural similarities between African American and Appalachian White Southern migrants.

(7) It's more being poor than the skin. Crackling bread. That's what people up here consider a Black thing. We ate that growing up. The other thing I thought was funny... a Black lady at church put a pair of silk undies at night to keep her hair in shape. My mom did that. It's not Black. People up here think we (Southerners) are dumb hicks every way you put it. Even in the South we're discriminated against by city people. Any minority group, regardless of race, has been treated wrongly. It's not just the color of your skin. But Blacks can't get away from it... Their skin color separates them no matter what. I've never had a racist bone in my body. We're all God's children. I don't have a racist bone in my body. (Speaker 12, Appalachian White F, b. 1965)

Speaker 12 also highlights a key difference between the situation of African American Southern migrants and Appalachian Whites when she acknowledges that "Blacks can't get away from it... Their skin color separates them no matter what." Indeed, many Southern Whites, including all but one of the Appalachian participants in this study, were eventually able to dissolve into the suburban landscape; Detroit African Americans, in contrast, have never penetrated the suburbs in a significant way (Farley *et al.* 2000). Speaker 8 is the one Appalachian White who remained in the inner city.

Bridget: Did you grow up in an integrated neighborhood?

Of course, I grew up with Black people!... We lived in Detroit. (Speaker 8, Appalachian White F, b. 1960)

This section demonstrated that African American and Appalachian White Southern migrants are salient to each other in the city/neighborhood landscape, more so historically than presently, since most Appalachian migrants have moved to the suburbs. Nevertheless, the presence of both African American and White Southern migrants in the city was frequently mentioned in the interviews.

8.2.5 Identification as "Southern" and "Hillbilly" and differentiation between Southern migrants and Midwestern Whites

Considering the common practice in sociolinguistics of ignoring or dismissing the role of regional identity in patterns of use for AAE until recently (Wolfram 2007), it is important to highlight that African American participants frequently identified themselves as "Southern" in the fieldwork phase of the study. Four years of participant observation in a Detroit African American community, in addition to the interviews, provided an ethnographic context to this self-identification as Southern. The Detroit African Americans in this study maintain a variety of Southern cultural traditions as well as ties to the South. Comments (1) and (2) are examples of self-identification as Southern by African American participants.

(1) Southerners still raise their gardens in Detroit... like we got a garden here (Speaker 1, African American F, b. 1927)

(2)... A lot of people from the South are up here, and we barbeque on our front porches. (Speaker 4, African American F, b. 1974)

Comment (3) provides an example of an Appalachian Southern migrant identifying as "hillbilly" (see also Comment (7) in Section 8.2.6 for an example of an African American participant using that term to label the dialect spoken by Appalachian migrants). Self-categorization as "Southern" to mean Southern African American and "hillbilly" to mean Appalachian White may be a form of ethnic differentiation in Detroit, but that remains open for a more large-scale study.

> (3) Oh, I just love it down South. People are much more friendlier. (Speaker 9, Appalachian White F, b. 1951)

> Bridget: Do you consider yourself a Southerner or a mixture?

> Actually, I consider myself a Southerner more so than a Northerner. No doubt about it. Southern cooking—that's all I do. I just made fried taters and pinto beans. My granddaughter loves fried okra and greens. We had them last week. Most people ask, "Are you a hillbilly"? And I say, "Yeah, I'm a hillbilly. I sure am." I'm not ashamed of it. I'd like to move back down South, but unfortunately my kids all work in the factories up here, in Chrysler. Most of them, so . . . I'd never leave my grandkids. I think that's why my mom's never gone back home, doesn't want to leave the grandkids. But I like it down South; its really peaceful and its . . . back home. We lived Downtown Detroit when we first got up here. Every hillbilly that's ever come to Detroit lived in the Southwest side. There's still a lot of people down there. Yeah there's a lot of Southern people down there. We lived there, but we eventually moved out this way. Lot of Southerners there. A lot of Southerners up here. (Speaker 9, Appalachian White F, b. 1951)

Another important component of the ethnographic analysis concerns comments that explicitly address differentiation between Southern migrants and Midwestern Whites (sometimes referred to as "Yankees" by the participants in this study), as in comment (4).

> (4) There is such a difference (from Southerners) in the way a typical Yankee thinks and the way they do things. People from up here are Yankees. . . . The true typical Yankees know it alls look down on you . . . That type . . . gives them a bad image . . . The pushy, impatient people. They treat Southern people like they're totally stupid, and they're used to a fast pace. But it's weird how those prejudices are, we get, I get tickled. [husband's name omitted] sister, she's married to someone up here who in my opinion is typical Yankee, you know. We kind of tolerate him

because we have to, but their kids are so Southern it's pathetic. And [name of her sister-in-law omitted] parents are typical, typical, what we consider Yankees, you know, and they're just... And so there's just such a difference in the way they think and the way they do things. (Speaker 12, Appalachian White F, b. 1965)

Speaker 5 describes a perception in comment (5) in which some African Americans in Detroit are different from African Americans she knows in the South.

(5) I really, really feel so strong about this..... And when you compare these people (in Michigan)... to African American people in... Southern states... that you will find that people in Southern states are more inclined to go to school, to get degrees because people did fight and lose their lives for the right to go to school. I think that's what I have a problem with most. (Speaker 5, African American F, b. 1974)

There are also comments contrasting sociocultural practices of the South with those of the North.

(6) In the South people go to the fellowship hall in church for dinners and wedding receptions. I don't go to church in Michigan, but I bet they go out to brunch afterwards in a restaurant. (Speaker 7, Appalachian White F, b. 1927)

(7) In Franklin (North Carolina), it is a time to visit with your neighbor. If you did that here, they'd carry you out by your neck. We don't talk about religion here (in Michigan). There are lots of differences between North and South. (Speaker 10, Appalachian White F, b. 1936)

Speaker 9 comments on differences as she perceives them between Southern and Midwestern gender roles for women (note again the use of the label "Yankee").

(8) Southerners visit; Yankees don't.... I was raised to take care of my husband and my children, to cook for them. My sons' wives are from up here, and they don't even cook. It all goes back to your

values, what you are raised with. . . . I love it down South. People are much more friendlier, more laid back. (Speaker 9, Appalachian White F, b. 1951)

The following comments highlight the differences between rural and urban cultures.

(9) It wouldn't have been quite as difficult, but being from the country, it seems like there's a lot of people here in the big city and I'm too much of a coward to drive, hard to get around. (Speaker 12, Appalachian White F, b. 1965)

(10) It's (the South is) a different world. It's at a different pace. I think that it's much more honest, maybe because it's the Bible Belt. Much more religious, more honest. I don't lock my doors (in the South). I dislike the city. When I came back to Michigan (from North Carolina) and Jim and I got married, I said, "I can't live like this, where you pull up in a driveway and there's a house on each side," you know forty feet apart or something. . . I have to have it open, can't be staring at my neighbor. . . I don't want that. I got displaced. (Speaker 10, Appalachian White F, b. 1936)

(11) I love the country. I don't like the city. (Speaker 2, African American F, b. 1936)

This section described social identification and differentiation for the Southern migrant participants. The next section provides meta-pragmatic commentary on language by the Southern migrant participants.

8.2.6 Metapragmatic commentary on language

This section showcases examples of metapragmatic commentary on language in the interview corpus. Comment (1) demonstrates an awareness of different expectations for greetings between Southerners and non-Southerners.

(1) Down South when people ask you how you are they want a couple of sentences where you tell them how you are. In Michigan, people ask but don't want you to really answer them. If I run into somebody in Michigan and they ask how I am it is a cliché.

In Franklin (North Carolina), it would be insulting to answer the same way as in Michigan. In Franklin, I have to give them fifteen seconds of how I am, and strangers speak to you. Here people are suspicious if you speak and they don't know you, "what does she want?" (Speaker 10, Appalachian White F, b. 1949)

Although Speaker 9 is a second-generation Southern migrant who has lived her entire life in the Detroit metropolitan area, she still perceives of herself as having a Southern accent.

(2) I don't think you ever lose a Southern accent. I don't think you ever really lose it. I think it's who you're around. (Speaker 9, Appalachian White F, b. 1951)

Comment (3) is important because it demonstrates the social salience of Southern English in Detroit (and, more generally, within the broader context of General American English).

(3) You're IQ goes out the window as soon as you open your mouth. (Speaker 12, Appalachian White F, b. 1965)

Speaker 12 also discusses the way her 13-year-old daughter "talks (more) Southern" after her annual return from spending the summer in the South with relatives.

(4) We used to get tickled at her (their thirteen year old daughter)... She would talk Southern, not that she was teasing, but she liked it, and after she comes home, she says the words. I probably say them as much but I don't notice it.... His cousin that lived up here just moved back to Tennessee. We were really close to her... Platt... Are you familiar with the word platt? Everybody else calls it "braids" and we'd say something about "platting hair" and everybody else would look at you like you were probably crazy. (Speaker 12, Appalachian White F, b. 1965)

Speaker 12 provides explicit commentary on the socially salient /ai/ in the especially salient pre-voiceless context, which was analyzed as part of this study and discussed in Chapter 7.

(5) I know after we got up here, we had friends that he (her husband) knew and his name is Mike, so I had called him and I says "Mike" [maːk] and he says, "No Mac lives here", and I says, "No. Mike. [maːk]" And after I said it two or three times, I finally said "It's Donna!" I kept saying it over and over.... They look at you like you re a total lunatic. (Speaker 12, Appalachian White F, b. 1965)

Going back to one of the themes discussed in Section 8.2.5, we see the label "hillbilly," this time applied to language.

(6) Yours (accent) is a lot stronger than mine. If I go down South, I come back with it stronger. Sometimes my husband says I talk like a hillbilly. You never really lose it. (Speaker 9, Appalachian White F, b. 1951)

One of the most important comments in the entire study was made by Speaker 2, an elderly African American participant. Speaker 2 stated that two dialects were to be found in the inner city of Detroit: African American English, which she refers to as "Southern," and Southern Appalachian, which she refers to as "Hillbilly":

(7) I have a heavy Southern accent, although I wasn't born in the South. A lot of the words I say come out with a very Southern accent. Then we also got what I call the hillbilly sound in Detroit, and we often mock one another. There's some good hillbillies here. (Speaker 2, African American F, b. 1936)

Metapragmatic commentary on language is important to the inter-pretation of the results presented in Chapters 6 and 7. Section 8.3 gives the interpretation of these results.

8.3   Interpretation of the results for the patterns of use presented in Chapters 6 and 7

Chapter 2 described language ideologies (see Section 2.2.2) as socially positioned beliefs about language and its relationship with society and culture. Johnstone (2003: 199) describes language ideology as " . . . people's beliefs about what language is, what is for, and what its roles in their lives should be." Language ideologies are manifested not only as reactions (or lack of reaction as the case may be) and attitudes to linguistic varieties and features, but also in patterns of use (Anderson and Milroy MS). These ideologies can change over time and space as particular groups (and particular linguistic features) shift in and out of salience. Since a change in language ideology can result in a change in a pattern of use, ideology shapes the direction of linguistic change (Anderson and Milroy MS). This approach contrasts with that of Labov (1994), in which linguistic change in vowel systems results primarily from language internal factors operating in a manner that is for the most part independent of the cultural orientations of individual speakers (see Section 2.2.1).

Chapter 2 described a "crucial site" as a culturally defined area in which "powerful ideological work is being done" (Phillips 2000: 233), a notion which I argue extends to the vowel space and vowel changes. The "work" in this context includes the marking of ethnolinguistic boundaries and the declaration of cultural affiliations. Linguistic features that are socially salient and show consistent patterns of differentiation between groups, as well as between individuals, constitute crucial sites for the expression of such ideologies. The nature of language ideologies cannot be determined simply by correlating linguistic features with social features determined by the researcher. As discussed in Chapter 2, analysis of linguistic variation in this framework requires that one attempt to identify the social categories that are most relevant to the participants. These categories may or may not mirror the conventional triumvirate of race, gender, and class.

The demographic and ethnographic evidence revealed in the participant comments above suggests that the relevant social opposition for contemporary Detroit African Americans is with Midwestern White speakers. The participant comments in Sections 8.1 and 8.2 on their own social and linguistic practices are relevant to the interpretation of the acoustic results presented in Chapters 6 and 7. Residential segregation in the city was salient to the Detroit African Americans whom I interviewed (discussed in Section 8.1), and a general cultural orientation to the South emerged during the fieldwork phase of the study (discussed in Section 8.2). Such comments provide evidence of sensitivity to the effects of residential segregation, and some participants reported that the only White people living in the city with them were Appalachians. In the context of the commentary on the saliency of residential segregation, it makes sense that African American speakers would index a strong linguistic boundary with Midwestern Whites. This is particularly relevant to the expansion of glide-weakened /ai/'s territory to the pre-voiceless phonetic environment; more on this is discussed in Section 8.3.2.

As noted above, a general orientation to Southern culture in Detroit was demonstrated by many of the participants. For example, all participants reported their families' pre-migration places of origin in the South, and many migrants, as well as Detroit-born descendants of migrants, described themselves and the culture of Detroit as "Southern." Participants often described neighborly visits, barbecues, pig-pickings, and other quintessential Southern activities as evidence of "Southernness." The Detroit African American and the Appalachian White participants frequently expressed a strong cultural loyalty to the South in their interviews, as revealed by the speaker comments in Section 8.2. The participant comments provide evidence that both the Appalachian White and African American participants in this study show a regional affiliation and cultural orientation to the South in addition to a linguistic one (pre-voiceless /ai/ glide-weakening), even if they are second or third-generation migrants. Several participants plan to move back South. Others expressed a desire to move back South but said they could not because they did not want to leave behind family in Detroit.

8.3.1   /u/ and /ʊ/

This section summarizes the results for the acoustic analysis of /u/ and /ʊ/. An important empirical finding is that the Detroit African American participants in this study show consistent fronting of /u/ and /ʊ/. Fronting of these vowels has generally been reported in the literature as characteristic only of White speakers (Labov 1994, 2001; Thomas 2001), with a few recent exceptions (Wolfram and Thomas 2002; Fridland 2003; Childs 2005). As Bailey and Thomas (1998) point out, fronting of these vowels has indexed Black and White ethnicity in the South and, according to Thomas (2001), in many areas still does. The results presented here, along with the pervasiveness of /u/ and /ʊ/ fronting generally, suggest that these changes no longer define either regional variation or, contrary to previous reports, Black and White ethnicity. I argue that in contrast with some areas of the South that still show a division along ethnic lines for this change (Thomas 2001), /u/ and /ʊ/ do not currently provide an ethnolinguistic boundary marker for either regional or ethnic identity for the participants in this study.

8.3.2 Comparison of groups for fronting

Chapter 6 reported patterns of fronting of /u/ and /ʊ/ for (1) the African American and Appalachian White Southern migrant participants in this study; (2) contemporary Detroit African American and 1966 African American speakers in Jennifer Nguyen's (2006) study; and (3) contemporary Detroit African American and Detroit White participants in Nguyen and Anderson (2006). Since these studies all employed the same acoustic methods, cross-comparisons of results yields a very clear picture of context-based fronting of /ʊ/ and /u/ in the Detroit metropolitan area.

The patterns for /ʊ/ across the data sets include the following: Nguyen (2006) reports context-based fronting for Wolfram's 1966 middle-class Detroit African American speakers in which pre-alveolar tokens are more fronted than pre-velar ones. Working-class 1966 African American speakers, however, show no fronting for /ʊ/. Nguyen's contemporary sample of Detroit African Americans spanning the entire social status spectrum shows the same pattern of context-based fronting as Wolfram's 1966 middle-class Detroit African American speakers. My study reports the same pattern of context-based fronting for Detroit African American Southern migrant participants as well as Appalachian White Southern migrant participants. When considered within the context of Nguyen's real-time data, it is clear that fronting of /ʊ/ in Detroit African American speech is a change in progress that happened first for middle-class African American speakers which is now reported for contemporary African American speakers of all social status levels in my study, Nguyen's (2006) study, and in a comparative study of Detroit African American and Detroit White speech (Nguyen and Anderson 2006), which show that this pattern of contextually based fronting also exists in the speech of White Detroiters. The current study cannot address whether /ʊ/ fronting is unrelated across the different communities in the Detroit area, or whether it may be a result of dialect contact.

Patterns of /u/ fronting are also contextually conditioned. The Detroit African American and Appalachian White Southern migrant participants in the current study show a pattern in which pre-alveolar /u/ is fronted relative to the position of pre-labial tokens of /u/, which are backed, and pre-word-boundary tokens, which fall in the middle of the two extremes of the front-back dimension of the vowel space. The same pattern is reported in Nguyen and Anderson (2006), which compares patterns of /u/ fronting for Detroit African American and Detroit White speakers. Both the African American and the Detroit White participants in that study show contextually conditioned fronting in which pre-alveolar variants are the most fronted and pre-labial variants are the most backed, but African American participants show greater contextually based fronting and backing than the Detroit White participants. Pre-word boundary tokens, as in the current study, fall in the middle of the two extremes. All of these groups showed more fronted variants of pre-alveolar /u/ than the Kalamazoo female participants in the Hillenbrand *et al.* (1995) study, which was used to make a baseline comparison between the backed pre-alveolar variants in that study and the fronted pre-alveolar variants for the Detroit participants. Unfortunately, Nguyen (2006) did not analyze /u/ so there is no real-time data for patterns of /u/ for Detroit African American speakers.

In the current study, the Southern migrant groups show strikingly similar context effects for their patterns of use; the only significant difference by ethnicity for the F_2 distance scores between the phonologically front and phonologically back vowels is that the African Americans show a more fronted pre-velar /ʊ/ than the Appalachian Whites. With regard to diphthongization, both groups showed a tendency for variants of /u/ to glide toward the back of the vowel space from midpoint to offset and for /ʊ/ to glide toward the front. I suggested in Section 6.3.3 that, in the case of /u/, this pattern of diphthongization may help to distinguish these variants from their front counterparts. Context effects from the following consonant allow for differentiation between groups of speakers. The Appalachian White and African American participants in this study show only subtle contextually conditioned differentiation; as noted above, the only environment that showed a significant difference by ethnicity for fronting scores was pre-velar /ʊ/. Section 4.3 described a similar pattern of subtle phonetic differentiation between Detroit African

American and Appalachian White speakers in which both groups tend to avoid /æ/-raising, but the African American speakers showed raising before pre-nasal following contexts.

As discussed in Section 6.2, context effects such as coarticulation are lawful and predictable, and as such different dialects should not show opposite directions for contextually conditioned changes. However, different dialects may well show different degrees for the progression as well as the limits on change. In this view, the earlier stages of a sound change are expected to show stronger contextual effects than the final stages. For example, for the Southern migrant speakers, /u/ shows strong conditioning effects from pre-alveolar and pre-labial following environments. The word-final variants, in contrast, fall in the middle of the two extremes (pre-alveolar promoting fronting and pre-labial inhibiting it). Contextually conditioned change progresses in an orderly fashion through environments: for example, pre-alveolar> pre-final> pre-labial for the fronting of /u/. Following environments whose acoustic and articulatory characteristics promote the change would show more advanced variants than environments which do not. For example, pre-alveolar contexts are amenable to fronting of the back vowels. Alveolar consonants are produced with a fronted tongue body; the acoustic consequence of this gesture is a high F_2. Back vowels, in contrast, show a backed tongue body and low F_2. The constriction must move forward in the front/back dimension of the articulatory space to produce an alveolar consonant after a back vowel. Labial consonants, which show a backed tongue body (and low F_2), inhibit fronting. The tongue body shows little or no movement going from a back vowel into a labial constriction. Rates of change, or progression through contexts, are expected to vary across dialects and individual speakers. In this view, a dialect (or an individual) showing strong contextual effects on fronting may eventually no longer show such conditioning after the change has progressed across contexts.

8.3.3 The (non)role of language ideology in the patterning of the high and lower-high back vowels

/u/ and /ʊ/ apparently are not the sites of significant sociolinguistic differentiation in the Detroit area—certainly not for the participants in this study and probably not in General American English since fronting of these vowels is a pervasive and wide-scale change.

Johnson (2003: 118) notes that /u/ generally tends to be fronted in American English. Nguyen and Anderson (2006) found that /u/ and /ʊ/ were fronted for contemporary Detroit AAE as well as for Detroit Whites, and, furthermore, both groups showed very similar patterns of contextual conditioning for the fronting process. Additional evidence that /u/ and /ʊ/ are not good candidates for being crucial ideological sites is that they do not seem to receive the same kinds of commentary as the socially stigmatized variants of /ai/ (discussed in Section 8.3.2; also see participant comment (5) in Section 8.2.6).

As noted above, what constitutes a crucial linguistic site is not contingent on linguistic factors alone and may vary across regions and time. In the South, fronting of high and lower-high back vowels among Whites and its absence among African Americans is apparently socially salient, prompting linguists to conclude that, for the most part, African Americans do not participate in this vowel change (e.g. Thomas 2001). As discussed in Section 2.1.5, the distinction between front and back variants of /u/ and /ʊ/ expresses a social meaning in the South, and at least until recently, African Americans are generally described as maintaining backed variants (Thomas 2001). Presumably, fronting of the high and lower-high back vowels is a more recent change for African Americans than for Whites. The reports indicating that African Americans participate in these widespread changes are recent (e.g. Fridland 2003; Childs 2005), but fronted variants of /u/ and /ʊ/ have been described as changes that have reached virtual completion in Southern White varieties (Labov 1994; Thomas and Bailey 1998; Thomas 2001).

I suggest that where the salient social division is along ethnic lines, as has been the case in the South, /u/ and /ʊ/ provide a crucial site for maintaining a linguistic boundary and expressing local meaning. The evidence from the previous section suggests that the African American participants in this study have experienced an ideological realignment following migration in which the primary distinction is between Northern Whites and Southern migrants rather than between Southern Blacks and Southern Whites. Because fronting of /u/ and /ʊ/ shows only subtle contextually conditioned differences between Black and White Southern migrant groups, I suggest that it has fallen from salience as a crucial linguistic site. The patterns of contextually conditioned fronting observed here can thus be understood as participation in a more global change in American English, contrary to the claims that African Americans do not participate in the widespread vowel rotations in American English (Labov 1994, 2001).

8.4 /ai/

While fronting of /u/ and /ʊ/ is apparently a global change, reported for varieties of English around the world (see Chapter 2), glide-weakening of /ai/ is a more restricted change associated in particular with speakers of Southern White varieties of English and AAE (Wolfram and Schilling-Estes 1998). Variation for /ai/ has been described as socially salient in American English (Wolfram and Schilling-Estes 1998: 75; Plichta and Preston 2003) and has played a different role than the high and lower-high back vowels as a socially meaningful linguistic boundary marker.

Besides being a more local change than fronting of the high and lower-high back vowels, another important difference between glide-weakened /ai/ and fronted back vowels is that the former does not show the lawful contextual conditioning of the latter. In other words, fronting of /u/ and /ʊ/ is constrained by universal phonetic (i.e. internal) factors, but /ai/ glide-weakening is not. In fact, from a phonetic point of view, it makes more sense for glide-weakening to occur first in pre-voiceless, rather than pre-voiced, contexts because pre-voiceless vowels show shorter durations. A vowel with a shorter duration is more amenable to truncation of the glide. The historical record for Southern variants of glide-weakened /ai/ indicate that, instead of what universal phonetic factors would lead us to predict, exactly the opposite scenario occurred, with pre-voiced contexts showing glide-weakening sooner than the pre-voiceless ones.

Glide-weakened variants of /ai/ (in pre-voiced and word-final contexts) are characteristic of both Southern White and African American varieties of English, varieties which have shared this feature for at least 100 years (Bailey and Thomas 1998). These variants distinguished Southern from non-Southern varieties of English, but did not distinguish Southern White from Southern African American varieties, at least until recently. Glide-weakening of /ai/ before voiceless obstruents is a more recent change (e.g. in Appalachian and Texan varieties) that AAE speakers are generally said not to participate in (Bailey and Thomas 1998: 104; Thomas 2001). The progression of glide-weakened variants of /ai/ to the pre-voiceless context for the Detroit African American participants is analyzed in Section 8.3.2 as a case of dialect leveling. Leveling is a typical linguistic response to speaker migration and mobility and subsequent dialect contact (see also Section 2.2.3). The evidence presented in Chapter 7 suggests that the Detroit African American speakers in this study have undergone a process of allophonic leveling that, while bringing their patterns into alignment with the Appalachian speakers, indexes a strong contrast with the Midwestern Whites. It seems that external, rather than internal, factors conditioned this change; this is in contrast to the fronting of /u/ and /ʊ/, which are conditioned by the internal contextual factor of following phonetic environment.

8.4.1 Summary of major patterns for /ai/

Diphthongal productions of /ai/ before pre-voiceless following contexts, as in [nais] "nice" and [lait] "light," is a pattern of use that is still in operation in conservative Southern White and conservative Southern AAE varieties. In other words, the reported pattern for General Southern White varieties and AAE is for there to be spectral differences based on voicing of the following consonant in which the diphthongal variant occurs before voiceless obstruents. The spread of glide-weakened variants to pre-voiceless following contexts is a more recent change than pre-voiced weakening (Thomas 2001) and is mainly reported for the non-plantation regions of the American South, such as the Great Smoky Mountains of the Southern Appalachians (Anderson 1999; Childs 2005) and Texas (Thomas 2001).

Non-Southern varieties of American English also show spectral differences for /ai/ based on the voicing of the following consonant. For these varieties, offsets tend to show lower values for F_1 and higher ones for F_2 before voiceless consonants than before voiced ones (Thomas 2000; Moreton 2004). Thomas (1991, 1993) reports such spectral differences for speakers in Ohio. Results from perceptual research also show that /ai/ tokens with shorter durations, lower F_1 values, and higher F_2 values are more consistently identified as occurring before a pre-voiceless consonant than a pre-voiced one (Thomas 2000: 15). Thomas argues that listeners are able to use the offset spectral difference as a perceptual cue to the identity of the following consonant (16). Thomas points out that truncation, rather than more extreme diphthongization, would be expected for vowels in pre-voiceless contexts because these vowels should show shorter durations. He suggests that the spectral differences in the offsets of /ai/ are instead used by speakers to compensate for the shorter duration by "... exaggerating the glide gesture" (2). Moreton (2004) tests Thomas's hypothesis that diphthongs show hyperarticulation before voiceless consonants and found that offglides for /ai/ as well as /oi eɪ aʊ/ showed "more peripheral" F_1 and F_2 offglides before voiceless consonants for 16 American English speakers. This researcher also ran a perceptual test which showed that tokens of /ai/ (*tide/tight*) were more likely to be judged as occurring in the pre-voiceless context when they showed lower F_1, higher F_2, and a shorter duration. F_2 was the most important cue for the pre-voiced/pre-voiceless distinction. Moreton concludes that "... [-voice] is correlated with, and cued by, peripheralization of diphthong offglides." In summary, more extreme diphthongization in the pre-voiceless environment is not only a feature of traditional Southern varieties, but is characteristic of general American (i.e. non-glide weakening) varieties as well.

Context effects such as those discussed above make it clear that it is important to consider the phonetic dimensions of /ai/ glide-weakening in detail. In the approach taken here, /ai/ was compared to the reference vowel /ɑ/, which was expected to show little, if any, diphthongization. Twelve of the 13 speakers did show more movement for either F_1, F_2, or both for /ai/ than /ɑ/.

The two older African American speakers showed diphthongization of /ai/ in pre-voiceless contexts, the traditional pattern described in the literature. For the younger African American speakers, however, as well as for all the Appalachian White speakers, for whom voicing had a significant conditioning effect, pre-voiced variants showed greater diphthongization from midpoint to offset than pre-voiceless variants. This is in contrast to the spectral differences based on voicing of the following consonant which are described above for General American English and may be the result of the longer duration of vowels in the pre-voiced context. Finally, both Southern migrant groups showed more glide-weakening for /ai/ than the Detroit White woman (Speaker 13), who showed greater movement for F_2 than either of the Southern migrant groups. In Section 8.3.2, I suggest that the important finding that all but the oldest African American speakers show glide-weakening of /ai/ in the pre-voiceless context may be best understood as a case of dialect leveling.

8.4.2   /ai/ Glide-weakening and dialect leveling

Given the association of pre-voiceless glide-reduced variants of /ai/ with White Southern dialects, their apparent absence from Detroit AAE until relatively recently (Anderson 2002; Nguyen 2006), the large-scale migration of many of the Detroit African Americans from the South, and the social ties of Detroit African Americans with White Appalachians who also migrated from the South, it is likely that glide-weakening of /ai/ in the progressive pre-voiceless following context is a result of dialect contact following migration. Dialect contact processes have effects which cannot always be explained in terms of direct transmission of particular linguistic forms between speakers (Anderson 2002). Phonological leveling is a process which reduces allophonic differentiation and renders vowel systems more similar to each other. Anderson and Milroy (MS), citing Trudgill (1986: 98), note that socially marked or minority variants are most susceptible to elimination.

The elimination of the pre-voiceless diphthongal allophone of /ai/ for the younger and middle-aged Detroit African American speakers is a case of allophonic leveling. The spread of a glide-weakened variant to the pre-voiceless context in Detroit AAE indexes a contrastive identity with Midwestern Whites and a linguistic affiliation with the South. The overall effect is that Detroit AAE aligns with a progressive Southern vowel system for /ai/, including that of the Detroit Southern White community, while indexing an opposition with Northern Whites.

The social sensitivity to /ai/ is demonstrated in the extreme variability of diphthongization shown among the individual speakers. Speakers 1 and 2 (the older African Americans) show the traditional pattern of pre-voiceless diphthongization. The middle-aged and younger speakers show glide-weakening across voicing contexts and tend to show a greater degree of diphthongization in pre-voiced contexts than in pre-voiceless ones (see Section 7.2.4). The Appalachian White speakers also show variability of diphthongization across individual speakers. All the Southern migrant speakers—both African American and Appalachian White—show less diphthongization for /ai/ than Speaker 13, the Detroit White woman (see Section 7.2.3).

Section 2.1.4 described the use of the Southern glide-weakened variant of /ai/ as socially salient, both inside and outside of the South (Wolfram and Schilling-Estes 1998; Plichta and Preston 2003), one of those "linguistic practices... more likely to be talked about than others in metapragmatic commentary" (Phillips 2000: 233). Nguyen (2006: 88) also comments on the social salience of /ai/; she cites work by Rahman (2003, 2005) among African American improvisational comedians. Nguyen discusses Rahman's finding that portrayals of African American characters utilized glide-weakened variants of /ai/, but portrayals of markedly middle-class African American speakers utilize diphthongal productions of /ai/. Speaker 12 commented specifically on the salience of pre-voiceless /ai/ for her own speech (Section 8.2.6).

Pre-voiceless /ai/ glide-weakening is a stereotypical marker of Southern speech (Johnstone 2003: 200; Plichta and Preston 2003). The leveling of the diphthongal variant in the pre-voiceless context by the middle-aged and younger African American speakers is ideologically mediated. The changes affecting /ai/ in Detroit's Northern White neighborhoods follow very different trajectories, which Eckert (1996) demonstrates are also highly socially salient (see Section 3.6). One outcome of the changes in Detroit AAE is thus the maintenance of a strong linguistic boundary between Detroit AAE and Midwestern White speakers, and a further outcome is the emergence of the progressive pre-voiceless glide-weakened variant of /ai/, which indexes a regional and linguistic affiliation with the South, an affiliation shared with White Appalachian Southern migrants. The patterning of /ai/ can be interpreted with reference to the speaker comments in Sections 8.1 and 8.2 which revealed that the African American participants maintain a variety of Southern cultural practices and maintain ties to the South evident, in some cases, in plans to return to the South. The relevant social opposition for the Detroit African American participants in this study is not with the Appalachian Southern migrants but with Midwestern Whites who live in the suburbs. Although all of the Appalachian migrant speakers in this study but one were eventually able to move to the inner suburbs, some of the Detroit African American participants indicated that the only White people living with them in the inner city suburbs were White Appalachians. Speaker 8 is an Appalachian White Southern migrant in this study who remained in the inner city instead of moving to the suburbs. Hartigan (1999) conducted ethnographic fieldwork with Appalachian Whites in the central city, and he also described cordial relations between African Americans and Appalachian Whites in his study.

I am not suggesting that the leveling of the pre-voiceless allophone of /ai/ for the African American speakers is the result of direct day-to-day contact between African American and Appalachian White speakers. The migration of African Americans from the South to Detroit resulted in a massive upheaval and radical change to their social and linguistic contexts which resulted in the pre-voiceless diphthongal allophone of /ai/ becoming socially redundant. In the South, AAE pre-voiceless diphthongal /ai/ indexes an opposition with Southern White groups that use the variant, but it is no longer necessary for the Detroit AAE speakers to index this social opposition (Anderson 2002). Differentiation among different social and linguistic groups became salient following migration from the rural South to the urban Midwest, and these changes in social differentiation yielded changes in language ideologies, ideological stances (Nguyen 2006), language attitudes, patterns of use, and social indexing among speaker groups. The expansion of the Southern glide-weakened variant of /ai/ to the progressive pre-voiceless context for the middle-aged and younger African American participants is a linguistic reflex of a changed social differentiation following migration (Anderson 2002).

It is important to point out that, as noted in Chapter 5, this study takes a detailed ethnographic and detailed acoustic approach and is limited in terms of the small sample size in terms of speakers (6 African American and 6 Appalachian White Southern migrants). I am not claiming that the vowel patterns reported in this study are typical of all speakers of Detroit AAE. Nguyen found different patterns for /ai/ in her dissertation about middle-class African American speech in Detroit. Nguyen cross-compares the results of her study of vocalic variables for contemporary men and women over a wide social status spectrum with those of Anderson (2003), an earlier incarnation of the present study. For /ai/, Nguyen's speakers maintain spectral differences between pre-voiced and pre-voiceless following contexts, although she does note that /ai/ "may be becoming less diphthongal over time" (2006: 102). A particularly important finding is that the females in her study are diphthongal for pre-voiceless /ai/. She analyzes the differing results for pre-voiceless /ai/ between the two studies in terms of ideological stances articulated by the different sets of speakers for each study:

> Far from contradicting Anderson's results . . . my analysis is that the different results for (pre-voiceless) /ai/ in our studies reflect the different ideologies of the speakers in our samples. As several quotes from Anderson's speakers showed, the speakers in her sample expressed animosity toward Detroit and a cultural affinity toward the South. Anderson linked these ideological stances with the linguistic results she found, suggesting that the speakers in her sample index a Southern orientation through their use of glide reduction in voiceless contexts . . . (157)

The speakers in Nguyen's study " . . . do not share the hostility toward Detroit, nor the affinity for the South . . . " Nguyen suggests:

> if Anderson is correct in correlating her speakers' feelings toward Detroit and the South with their use of Southern White patterns of /ai/ glide reduction, then we would predict, based on my own speakers' lack of such expressed ideologies about Detroit and the South, that the speakers in my sample would not display the Southern White pattern of /ai/ glide-reduction. Thus, I suggest that the differences between my own results for /ai/ and those of Anderson (2003) . . . support Anderson's correlation between ideological stances and linguistic use. (158)

Eagleton (1991: 9) describes ideology as "(concerning) the actual uses of language between particular human subjects for the production of specific effects" and as a " . . . function of the relation of an utterance to its social context." As Eagleton points out, an important factor to consider when trying to understand the role of ideology encoded in language is " . . . a question of who is saying what to whom for what purposes" (9). In other words, it is important to consider the context of the interview event when interpreting the patterns reported in the analysis chapters. Participants were asked to tell me about their everyday experiences in Detroit and to comment on changes they had witnessed in Detroit in their lifetimes. The social salience of topics centering on perceptions of the South and being Southern emerged during the course of fieldwork. Eagleton also addresses the role of context:

> It may help to view ideology less as a particular set of discourses, than as a particular set of effects within discourses.... (Its) effects are discursive, not purely formal, features of language. What is interpreted will depend on the concrete context of the utterance, and it is variable from one communicative situation to the next (194).... Ideology offers a set of reasons for material conditions (209).... A person's "real" situation is inseparably bound up with linguistic interpretation of one kind or another. (213)

The ideological stances evident in the comments for the African American participants on the topics of life in the inner city, residential segregation, and important historical events such as the "White Flight" and the 1967 riot reflect the material conditions of these speakers and provide a context for the differentiation, both culturally and linguistically, between the African American Southern migrants and Midwestern Whites. This is particularly evident in the patterning of the highly socially salient glide-weakened /ai/. The African American and Appalachian White Southern migrant participants in this study show very different patterns of use for /ai/ than those described by Eckert (2000) for non-Southern suburban Whites as well those described by Nguyen (2006) for her sample of Detroit African Americans who did not report frustration with inner city life, as the participants in my study did, or an affiliation with the South. More generally, /ai/ is salient within the broader context of American English (Wolfram and Schilling-Estes 1998).

9
Conclusions and Implications

9.1 General commentary

Section 2.2 discusses Labov's claim that large-scale vowel changes are largely structured by language internal principles (Labov 1994). In his second volume on language change, he suggests that, for the most part, "social and structural elements in language (are) segregated" (Labov 2001: 29). In short, he conceptualizes internal and external types of change as two very different creatures which rarely interact:

> ... internal and external (factors) are effectively independent of each other. If an internal factor is dropped or changed, changes appear in other internal factors, but the external factors remain unchanged; if an external factor is dropped or changed, other external factors change but the internal factors remain as they were. These basic sociolinguistic findings provide the methodological rationale for ... the separate discussion of internal and external factors. (Labov 1994: 3)

Chapter 8 considered internal constraints on the fronting of the high and lower-high back vowels as well as the external motivations driving the allophonic leveling of diphthongal variant of /ai/ in the progressive pre-voiceless context. I have argued that some vowel changes, such as /ai/ glide-weakening in the pre-voiceless context, provide a crucial site for indexing an allegiance to the South and an opposition with Midwestern Whites, while the other change examined in this study, fronting of /u/ and /ʊ/, does not constitute a site for social and linguistic differentiation in Detroit (see also Nguyen and Anderson 2006). Insisting that only language internal principles structure vowel rotations in American English cannot explain these patterns; nor does it have sufficient explanatory power to account for why African American speakers show different reactions over time and space to widespread changes such as /u/ and /ʊ/ fronting and regional changes such as pre-voiceless /ai/ glide-weakening. In the South, African Americans are most typically characterized as avoiding both of these changes (Labov 2001; Thomas 2001), but recent studies, including Fridland (2003), Wolfram and Thomas (2002), and Childs (2005) indicate that at least some African Americans in the South do participate in these changes. Likewise, the Detroit African Americans in this study participate in both of these changes which were previously described as characteristic of Whites only. Although fronting of the back vowels shows strong contextual conditioning (i.e. are internally constrained), the process is also subject to ideological intervention. This could explain why at least some African Americans in the South do not show fronting of the high and lower-high back vowels or pre-voiceless /ai/ glide-weakening (Thomas 2001). In those areas, where the salient division is along ethnic lines, backing for /u/ and /ʊ/ remains a crucial site. Interestingly, it is these linguistically conservative areas of the South (formally the plantation region of the South), where Blacks and Whites show similar patterns of /ai/ glide-weakening in that both groups maintain the diphthong in the pre-voiceless context (Wolfram and Schilling-Estes 1998; Thomas 2001). In those areas, it seems that /u/ and /ʊ/ are crucial sites for ethnic boundary marking while /ai/ is not. Recall from Section 2.1.4 that glide-weakening in the pre-voiceless context is a progressive change reported for restricted groups of speakers (e.g. in Texas as well as the Smoky Mountain region of North Carolina and East Tennessee). For the African Americans in Detroit and elsewhere that show fronting, /u/ and /ʊ/ have lost their social salience, that is their local meaning, and no longer constitute a crucial site for the expression and maintenance of local language ideologies. /ai/, in contrast, is rich in local meaning for both groups of Southern migrant speakers and Southern speakers generally (Wolfram and Schilling-Estes 1998; Plichta and Preston 2003; Tillery and Bailey 2003). /ai/ also shows a different trajectory of change for White speakers in the suburbs, and is highly socially salient there as well (Eckert 2000).

As noted above, there are important sociolinguistic differences between fronting of /u/ and /ʊ/ and /ai/ glide-weakening. While fronting of /u/ and /ʊ/ are widespread, perhaps even global, changes in varieties of English, glide-weakening of /ai/ is a more local change associated with specific groups of people, namely African Americans and some groups of Southern Whites. /ai/ has been described as socially salient by many sociolinguistic researchers, including several who have conducted research in Detroit (Deser 1990; Eckert 1996; Edwards 1997). Social sensitivity to /ai/ is also expressed through the extreme variability in the vowel realizations across speakers. This is hardly surprising because it is a highly socially salient vowel feature of Southern speech (Plichta and Preston 2003); also, Southern speech in general is highly socially salient (Preston 1996; Johnstone 2003). Fronting of /u/ and /ʊ/ does not carry this kind of social significance or receive this kind of public commentary; these are widespread vowel changes affecting not just Southern varieties, but many varieties, of American English (Labov 1994, 2001; Thomas 2001), including General American English (Johnson 2003). Accordingly, fronted realizations of /u/ and /ʊ/ do not appear to be crucial sites for the expression of a local language ideology for the Detroit African American speakers in this study. Finally, the two sets of changes are different in that fronting of /u/ and /ʊ/ is internally constrained by contextual effects from the following consonants. /ai/ glide-weakening, in contrast, does not seem to follow a lawful, phonetically constrained path of change. It is a different sort of change, dialect leveling, a process which is frequently an outcome of language contact resulting from situations of migration and mobility (Milroy 2002).

9.2 Limitations and contributions of the study and implications for sociolinguistic research

This work, most certainly, does not represent the "last word" on AAE and Appalachian English in Detroit. I want to mention the limitations of this work. As discussed in Chapter 5, this study analyzes many tokens from a small number of speakers (13 speakers for the main part of the study; additional speakers were analyzed for the Pilot Study discussed in Chapter 4). Due to the "case study" approach taken here, I cannot make any large claims about Detroit speech or about Appalachian English or AAE in a broad sense. Rather, I describe the linguistic behavior of the Southern migrant participants in this study. My claims are focused on their speech alone. I do not regret taking the approach I chose. The depth-first approach allowed me to analyze enough tokens (5859, to be exact) to understand the role of phonetic context in shaping (more specifically, constraining) the patterns of language use described in this study for the high and lower-high back vowels. I hope I have demonstrated the importance of considering phonetic context in discussions of language variation in American English. The expense of a detailed acoustic analysis, as I have said, is that it limited the number of speakers I was able to include in the analysis. Finally, I want to acknowledge the vital importance of large-scale studies of speech communities, such as those conducted by Walt Wolfram and his students as well as the studies of Bill Labov and his students; the methodology in this study aims only to supplement these more traditional approaches.

I also want to acknowledge that studying language ideology presents its own unique set of challenges. Since I did not specifically attempt to obtain metapragmatic commentary on the vowels in this study (I did not even know what vowels I would study when I began the fieldwork), I am not able to operationalize ideology in any concrete way, as pointed out by John Baugh (personal communication). The analysis appeals to a language ideological interpretive framework, based on a framework developed by linguistic anthropologists (see further Chapter 2), in a general, not a specific, way. Eagleton (1991) defines ideology, in the general sense, as "any set of beliefs motivated by social interests" (2). I have tried to reveal key beliefs and participant interpretations of life in the Detroit metropolitan area as encoded in commentary from individual participants. I argue in particular that belief and attitudes shape language use by creating social oppositions such as Southern/Midwestern White and Inner City Detroit/Suburban Detroit, social oppositions that are reflected in linguistic differentiation, such as the differentiation between groups in Detroit for patterns of use for the socially salient /ai/ vowel (see also Eckert 2000). However, I fully acknowledge the slippery nature of ideology as reflected in language or any other social behavior, and my claims concerning language ideology should be understood as being tentative claims.

Despite its limitations, I hope this book has made contributions to the study of language variation and American English vowel systems.

This study has presented several methodological innovations (see further Anderson 2003) which can be applied to future studies. The goals of these methods are to allow cross-speaker comparisons and facilitate replication by other researchers. For /u/ and /ʊ/, I have quantified fronting not simply through analysis of absolute F_2 measurements, which vary substantially across speakers, but rather by measuring the differences in F_2 between /u/ and /i/ and between /ʊ/ and /ɪ/. This relative measure acknowledges that the notion of fronting only has meaning in reference to the front of the vowel space, as defined by the F_2 values of the front vowels. The findings also demonstrate the need to consider effects of following context, which are not generally analyzed in socioacoustic work on varieties of American English. Diphthongization is also a relative notion, which can best be quantified with reference to a non-diphthongal vowel such as /ɑ/. I have demonstrated a method for precisely quantifying diphthongization of /ai/ by subtracting F_1 and F_2 midpoint values from offset values. These measurements make it possible to specify both the length and direction of the glide.

This project has also indicated several fruitful directions for future research. The clear-cut contextual effects on the patterns of use for /u/ and /ʊ/ suggest that socioacoustic work on vowel systems should consider context effects such as coarticulation. Based on the results for this study, I would predict global, or frequently attested, changes to show contextual conditioning at least in the earlier stages of change. More established changes presumably show less contextual conditioning. Different dialects and different speakers would not be expected to show opposite patterns of shifting, but the rate of change across environments could vary. Finally, future research should also address the question of the degree to which African Americans are participating in widespread (which are not just "Whitespread") vowel changes in American English.

Bibliography

Akers, Elmer. 1936. *Southern Whites in Detroit.* Ph.D. Dissertation. University of Michigan, Ann Arbor.

Anderson, Bridget L. 1997. "Adaptive sociophonetic strategies and dialect accommodation: /ay/ monophthongization in Cherokee English." *University of Pennsylvania Working Papers in Linguistics* 4(1): 185–202.

——. 1998. *An Acoustic Study of Phonological Transfer and Vowel Accommodation among the Snowbird Cherokee.* Master's Thesis, North Carolina State University, Raleigh, NC.

——. 1999. "Source-language transfer and vowel accommodation in the patterning of Cherokee English /ai/ and /oi/." *American Speech* 74(4): 339–368.

——. 2001. "Phonetic variants are important in phonological processes." *Linguistic Society of America Annual Meeting*, Washington, DC.

——. 2002. "Dialect leveling and /ai/ monophthongization among African American Detroiters." *Journal of Sociolinguistics* 6(1): 86–98.

——. 2003. *An Acoustic Study of Southeastern Michigan Appalachian and African American Southern Migrant Vowel Systems.* Ph.D. Dissertation. University of Michigan.

——. In press. "A quantitative acoustic approach to /ai/ glide weakening among Detroit African American and Appalachian White Southern Migrants." *Language and Variety in the South III: Historical and Contemporary Perspectives.* Tuscaloosa: University of Alabama Press.

Anderson, Bridget L. and Mark Arehart. 2001. "Creaky voice and the Detroit AAE vowel system." *New Ways of Analyzing Variation 30*, Raleigh, NC.

Anderson, Bridget L. and Valerie Fridland. 2002. "A comparative study of /ai/ among African Americans in Memphis and Detroit." *New Ways of Analyzing Variation 31*, Stanford, CA.

Anderson, Bridget L. and Lesley Milroy. 1999. "Southern sound changes and the Detroit African American English vowel system." *New Ways of Analyzing Variation 28*, Toronto.

——. 2001a. "Towards an integrated account of internal and external constraints on language change." *Linguistic Society of America Annual Meeting*, Washington, DC.

——. 2001b. "Detroit Southern Migrant varieties of English and the Northern Cities Shift." *New Ways of Analyzing Variation 30*, Raleigh, NC.

——. Unpublished manuscript. *Internal and External Constraints on Change in the Detroit African American Vowel System: A Case Study and Some Further Implications*, The University of Michigan.

Anderson, Bridget L., Lesley Milroy, and Jennifer Nguyen. 2002. "Fronting of /u/ and /ʊ/ among Detroit African Americans: Evidence from real and apparent time." *New Ways of Analyzing Variation 31*, Stanford, CA.

Ash, Sharon. 1996. "Freedom of movement: /uw/-fronting in the Midwest." In Jennifer Arnold, Reneé Blake, Brad Davidson, Scott Schwenter, and Julie Soloman, eds. *Sociolinguistic Variation: Data, Theory, and Analysis: Selected Papers from NWAV 23 at Stanford*. Stanford University: Center for the Study of Language and Information. 162–175.

Bailey, Guy and Erik Thomas. 1998. "Some aspects of AAVE phonology." In Salikoko S. Mufwene, John R. Rickford, Guy Bailey, and John Baugh, eds. *African-American English: Structure, History, and Use*. London: Routledge. 85–109.

Bailey, Guy, Tom Wikle, Jan Tillery, and Lori Sand. 1996. "The consequences of catastrophic events: An example from the American Southwest." In Jennifer Arnold, Reneé Blake, Brad Davidson, Scott Schwenter, and Julie Soloman, eds. *Sociolinguistic Variation: Data, Theory, and Analysis*. Stanford, CA: Center for the Study of Language and Information.

Beckford, Alicia. 1999. *A Sociophonetic Analysis of Jamaican Vowels*. Ph.D. Dissertation. University of Michigan, Ann Arbor.

Beddor, Patrice Speeter, James D. Harnsberger, and Stephanie Lindemann. 2002. "Language-specific patterns of vowel-to-vowel coarticulation: Acoustic structures and their perceptual correlates." *Journal of Phonetics* 30: 591–627.

Bernstein, Cynthia and Elizabeth Gregory. 1993. "Measuring social causes of phonological variables." *American Speech* 68: 227–240.

——. 1994. "The social distribution of glide-shortened /ai/ in LAGS." *Southeastern Conference on Linguistics 50*. Memphis, TN.

Berry, Chad. 2000. *Southern Migrants: Northern Exiles*. Urbana and Chicago: University of Illinois Press.

Campbell, Lyle. 1999. *Historical Linguistics: An Introduction*. Cambridge, MA: MIT Press.

Chambers, Jack. 1992. "Dialect acquisition." *Language* 68(3): 673–705.

——. 1995. *Sociolinguistic Theory: Linguistic Variation and Its Social Significance*. Blackwell: Oxford.

Childs, Becky. 2005. *Investigating the Local Construction of Identity: Sociophonetic Variation in Smoky Mountain African American Women's Speech*. Ph.D. Dissertation. The University of Georgia.

Clarke, Sandra, Ford Elms, and Amani Youssef. 1995. "The third dialect of English: Some Canadian evidence." *Language Variation and Change* 7: 209–228.

Deser, Toni. 1990. *Dialect Transmission and Variation: An Acoustic Analysis of Vowels in Six Urban Detroit Families*. Ph.D. Dissertation. Boston University.

Dressler, W.U. and S. Moosmuller. 1991. "Phonetics and phonology: A socio-psycholinguistic framework." *Phonetica* 48: 135–148.

Eagleton, Terry. 1991. *Ideology: An Introduction*. London: Verso.

Eckert, Penelope. 1987. "Relative values of opposing variables." In K.M. Denning, S. Inkelas, F.C. Mc Nair-Knox, and J.R. Rickford, eds. *New Ways of Analyzing Variation 15*, Stanford, CA.

——. 1988. "Sound change and adolescent social structure." *Language in Society* 17: 183–207.

——. 1989. *Jocks and Burnouts: Social Categories and Identity in the High School.* New York: Teachers College Press.

——. 1991. "Social polarization and the choice of linguistic variants." In Penelope Eckert, ed. *New Ways of Analyzing Sound Change.* San Diego: Academic Press. 213–232.

——. 1996. "(ay) goes to the city: Reminiscences of Martha's Vineyard." In John Baugh, Crawford Feagin, Greg Guy, and Deborah Schriffrin, eds. *Towards a Social Science of Language: Festschrift for William Labov.* Philadelphia and Amsterdam: John Benjamins. 47–68.

——. 2000. *Linguistic Variation as Social Practice.* Oxford: Blackwell.

——. 2001. "Style and social meaning." In Penelope Eckert and John Rickford, eds. *Style and Sociolinguistic Variation.* Cambridge: Cambridge University Press.

Edwards, Walter. 1997. "The variable persistence of southern vernacular features in the speech of inner city black Detroiters." In Cynthia Bernstein, Thomas Nunally, and Robin Sabino, eds. *Language Variety in the South Revisited.* Tuscaloosa: University of Alabama Press. 76–86.

Elias, Katherine. M.S. *The Detroit System: A Report on the Social Geography and Demographic Structure of Detroit.* The University of Michigan.

Evans, Betsy. 2001. *Dialect Contact and the Northern Cities Shift in Ypsilanti, Michigan.* Ph.D. Dissertation. Michigan State University, Lansing.

Farley, Reynolds, Sheldon Danziger, and Harry Holzer. 2000. *Detroit Divided.* New York: The Russell Sage Foundation.

Fasold, Ralph. 1969. *A Sociolinguistic Study of the Pronunciation of Three Vowels in Detroit Speech.* Georgetown University mimeograph.

Foulkes, Paul and Gerald Docherty, eds. 1999. *Urban Voices: Accent Studies in the British Isles.* London: Arnold.

Frekko, Susan. Unpublished manuscript. *Detroit Project Participant Profiles.* The University of Michigan.

Fridland, Valerie. 1999. "The Southern Shift in Memphis, Tennessee." *Language Variation and Change* 11: 267–285.

——. 2001. "The relationship of network strength and changes in the Southern Vowel Shift among African Americans in Memphis, Tennessee." *New Ways of Analyzing Variation (NWAV) 30* , Raleigh, NC.

——. 2003. "Network strength and the realization of the Southern Vowel Shift among African-Americans in Memphis, TN." *American Speech* 78.

——. 2004. "Tied, tie and tight: /ay/ monophthongization among African-Americans and European-Americans in Memphis, TN." *Journal of Sociolinguistics.*

Gordon, Matthew. 1997. *Urban Sound Change Beyond City Limits: The Spread of the Northern Cities Shift in Michigan.* Ph.D. Dissertation. University of Michigan, Ann Arbor.

——. 2000. "Phonological correlates of ethnic identity: Evidence of divergence?" *American Speech* 75: 115–136.

——. 2001. *Small-Town Values, Big-City Vowels: A Study of the Northern Cities Shift in Michigan.* Durham, NC: Duke University Press.

Graff, David, William Labov, and Wendell A. Harris. 1986. "Testing listeners' reactions to phonological markers of ethnic identity: A new method for sociolinguistic research." In David Sankoff, ed. *Diversity in Diachrony.* Amsterdam Studies in the Theory and History of Linguistic Science, series 4, Current Issues in Linguistic Theory 53. Amsterdam: John Benjamins. 45–58.

Gregory, James N. 2005. *The Southern Diaspora: How the Great Migrations of Black and White Southerners Transformed America.* Chapel Hill: University of North Carolina Press.

Habick, Timothy. 1980. *Sound Change in Farmer City: A Sociolinguistic Study Based on Acoustic Data.* Ph.D. Dissertation. University of Illinois, Urbana-Champaign.

———. 1993. "Farmer City, Illinois: Sound systems shifting South." In Timothy C. Frazer, ed. *"Heartland" English: Variation and Transition in the American Midwest.* Tuscaloosa: University of Alabama Press. 97–124.

Hall, Joseph S. 1942. "The phonetics of Great Smoky Mountain speech." *American Speech Reprints and Monographs,* No. 4. New York: Columbia University Press.

Hartigan, John Jr. 1999. *Racial Situations: Class Predicaments of Whiteness in Detroit.* Princeton, NJ: Princeton University Press.

Hazen, Kirk and Ellen Fluharty. 2001. "Defining Appalachian English: Bidialectalism and beyond." *New Ways of Analyzing Variation 30,* Raleigh, NC.

Hillenbrand, James, Laura A. Getty, Michael J. Clark, and Kimberlee Wheeler. 1995. "Acoustic characteristics of American English vowels." *Journal of the Acoustical Society of America* 97(5): 3099–3111.

Irvine, Judith T. and Susan Gal. 2000. "Language ideology and linguistic differentiation." In Paul Kroskrity, ed. *Regimes of Language.* Santa Fe, NM: School of American Research Press. 35–84.

Johnson, Keith. 1989. "Higher formant normalization results from auditory integration of F2 and F3." *Perception and Psychophysics* 46: 174–180.

———. 2003. *Acoustic and Auditory Phonetics* (2nd edition). Oxford: Blackwell.

Johnstone, Barbara. 2000. "The individual voice on language." *Annual Review of Anthropology* 29: 405–424.

———. 2003. "Features and the use of southern style." In Stephen J. Nagle and Sara L. Sanders, eds. *English in the Southern United States.* Cambridge University Press. 159–172.

Jones, Jamila. Unpublished manuscript. *The Vowel Systems of African Americans in the Urban North.* Michigan State University.

Jones, Jamila and Dennis R. Preston. In press. "AAE and identity: Constructing and deploying linguistic resources." H. Samy Alim and John Baugh, eds. *Festschrift for Geneva Smitherman.* New York, NY: Routledge.

Kroskrity, Paul. 2000. "Regimenting languages: Language ideological perspectives." In Paul Kroskrity, ed. *Regimes of Language.* Santa Fe, NM: School of American Research Press. 1–34.

Kurath, Hans and Raven I. McDavid, Jr. 1961. *The Pronunciation of English in the Atlantic States.* Ann Arbor, MI: University of Michigan Press.

Labov, William. 1963. "The social motivation of sound change." *Word* 19: 273–309.

——. 1972. "Some principles of linguistic methodology." *Language in Society* 1: 97–120.

——. 1991. "The three dialects of English." In Penelope Eckert, ed. *Analysis of Sound Change in Progress.* New York, NY: Academic Press.

——. 1994. *Principles of Linguistic Change: Internal Factors.* Cambridge, MA: Basil Blackwell.

——. 1998. "Co-existent systems in African-American Vernacular English." In Salikoko S. Mufwene, John R. Rickford, Guy Bailey, and John Baugh, eds. *African-American English: Structure, History, and Use.* London: Routledge. 110–153.

——. 2001. *Principles of Linguistic Change: Social Factors.* Oxford: Blackwell.

Labov, William and Wendell A. Harris. 1986. "De Facto Segregation of Black and White vernaculars." In David Sankoff, ed. *Diversity and Diachrony.* Amsterdam Studies in the Theory and History of Linguistic Science, series 4, Current Issues in Linguistic Theory 53: 1–24.

Ladefoged, Peter. 1996. *Elements of Acoustic Phonetics.* Chicago: University of Chicago Press.

Lass, Roger. 1997. *Historical Linguistics and Language Change.* Cambridge: Cambridge University Press.

Lippi-Green, Rosina. 1997. *English with an Accent: Language, Ideology and Discrimination in the United States.* London: Routledge.

Luthin, Herbert W. 1987. "The story of California (ow): The coming-of-age of English in California." In Keith M. Denning, Sharon Inkelas, Faye C. McNair-Knox, and John C. Rickford, eds. *Variation in Language: NWAV-XV at Stanford. Proceedings of the Fifteenth Annual Conference on New Ways of Analyzing Variation.* Stanford, CA: Department of Linguistics, Stanford University. 312–324.

MacMahon, Michael. 1998. *Phonology.* The Cambridge history of the English language Volume IV; 1776–1997. Cambridge: Cambridge University Press. 373–535.

Mallinson, Christine, Walt Wolfram, and Jaclyn Fried. 2001. "Dialect accommodation in a bi-ethnic mountain enclave community: More evidence on the earlier development of African American English." *Southeastern Conference on Linguistics LXIV*, Knoxville, Tennessee.

Marckwardt, Albert H. 1957. *Principal and Subsidiary Dialect Areas in the North-Central States.* Publication of the American Dialect Society 27.

Marks, Carole. 1989. *Farewell—We're Good and Gone: The Great Black Migration.* Blacks in the Diaspora Series. Bloomington: Indiana University Press.

Metropolitan Area Employment and Unemployment Summary. Accessed via the internet at http://www.bls.gov/news.release/metro.nr0.htm

Milroy, James. 1992. *Linguistic Variation and Change.* Oxford: Blackwell.

Milroy, Lesley. 1987a. *Observing and Analyzing Natural Language: A Critical Account of Sociolinguistic Methods.* Oxford: Blackwell.

——. 1987b. *Language and Social Networks.* Oxford: Blackwell.

——. 2002. "Introduction: Mobility, contact, and language change—working with contemporary speech communities." *Journal of Sociolinguistics* 6(1): 3–15.

Milroy, Lesley and Matthew Gordon. 2003. *Sociolinguistics: Methods and Interpretation.* Oxford: Blackwell.

Moreton, Elliott. 2004. "Realization of the English postvocalic [voice] contrast in F_1 and F_2 ." *Journal of Phonetics* 32: 1–33.

Munro, Murray J., Tracey M. Derwing, and James E. Flege. 1999. "Canadians in Alabama: A perceptual study of dialect acquisition in adults." *Journal of Phonetics* 27: 385–403.

Nguyen, Jennifer. 2006. *The Changing Social and Linguistic Orientation of the African American Middle Class.* Ph.D. Dissertation. University of Michigan.

Nguyen, Jennifer and Bridget Anderson 2006. "A comparison of /u/ and /ʊ/ fronting for African American and White Detroiters." *New Ways of Analyzing Variation (NWAV) 35*, Ohio State University.

Niedzielski, Nancy. 1999. "The effect of social information on the perception of sociolinguistic variables." *Journal of Language and Social Psychology* 18(1): 62–85.

Ohala, John. 1981. "The origin of sound patterns in vocal tract constraints." In Peter MacNeilage, ed. *The Production of Speech*. New York: Springer Verlag. 189–216.

———. 1992. "The segment: Primitive or derived?" In G.J. Docherty and D.R. Ladd, eds. *Papers in Laboratory Phonology II: Gesture, Segment, Prosody.* Cambridge: Cambridge University Press.

Parr, John. 1998. "Detroit: Struggling against history." In Bruce Adams & John Parr, eds. *Boundary Crossers: Case Studies of How Ten of America's Metropolitan Regions Work*. Academy of Leadership: The University of Maryland Press. Accessed via the internet, http://www.academy. umd.edu/Publications/boundary/CaseStudies/bcsdetroit.htm

Pederson, Lee. 1983. *East Tennessee Folk Speech.* New York: Verlag Peter Lang.

Peirce, Neil and Curtis Johnson. 1998. *Boundary Crossers: Community Leadership for a Global Age.* Academy of Leadership: The University of Maryland Press. Accessed via the internet, http://www.academy.umd. edu/Publications/boundary/CaseStudies/bcsdetroit.htm

Phillips, Susan U. 2000. "Constructing a Tongan Nation-State through language ideology in the courtroom." In Paul Kroskrity, ed. *Regimes of Language*. Santa Fe, NM: School of American Research Press. 229–257.

Pierrehumbert, Janet, Mary E. Beckman, and D.R. Ladd. 2001. "Conceptual foundations of phonology as a laboratory science." In N. Burton-Roberts, P. Carr, and G. Docherty, eds. *Phonological Knowledge: Its Nature and Status.* Oxford: Oxford University Press. 273–304.

Plichta, Bartek and Dennis Preston. 2003. "The /ay/s have it: Stereotype, perception, and region. *Paper presented at New Ways of Analyzing Variation 32*. University of Pennsylvania.

Preston, Dennis R. 1996. "Where the worst English is spoken." In Edgar Schneider, ed. *Focus on the USA*. Amsterdam: John Benjamins. 297–360.

Preston, Dennis R., Rika Ito, Evans, Betsy E., and Jamila Jones (2000). Change on top of change: Social and regional accommodation to the Northern Cities Chain Shift. In H. Bennis, H. Ryckeboer, and J. Stroop, eds. *De Toekomst van de Variatielinguitiek* (special issue of Taal en Tongval to honor Dr. Jo Daan on her ninetieth birthday ed., 61–86). Amsterdam: Meertens.

Rahman, Jacquelyn. 2003. "Golly gee! The construction of middle-class white characters in the monologues of African-American comedians." *New Ways of Analyzing Variation 32*, Philadelphia, PA.

——. 2005. "'Talking White at the Apollo': African American narrative comedians portraying the middle-class establishment." *American Dialect Society Annual Meeting*, Oakland, CA.

Repp, Bruce. 1982. "Categorical perception: Issues, methods, findings." *Haskins Laboratories Report on Speech Research* 70 (April–June): 99–183.

Schilling-Estes, Natalie. 1996. *The Linguistic and Sociolinguistic Status of /ay/ in Outer Banks English*. Ph.D. Dissertation. University of North Carolina, Chapel Hill.

——. 1997. "Accommodation versus concentration: Dialect death in two post-insular island communities." *American Speech* 72: 12–32.

——. 2000. "Inter-ethnic differentiation and cross-ethnic accommodation: /ay/ in Lumbee Native American Vernacular English." *Language Variation and Change* 3: 141–174.

SEMCOG (Southeastern Michigan Council of Governments). 1994. *Patterns of Diversity and Change in Southeast Michigan*. Detroit: Community Foundation.

Shuy, Roger, Walt Wolfram, and William K. Riley. 1968. *Field Techniques in an Urban Language Study*. Washington, DC: Center for Applied Linguistics.

Silverstein, Michael. 1979. "Language structure and linguistic ideology." In Paul R. Clyne, William F. Hanks, and Carol L. Hofbaur, eds. *In the Elements: A Parasession on Linguistic Units and Levels*. Chicago: Chicago Linguistics Society. 193–247.

——. 1992. "The uses and utility of ideology: Some reflections." *Pragmatics* 2: 311–323.

——. 1996. "Indexical order and the dialectics of social life." In Risako Ide, Rebecca Parker, and Yukako Sunaoshi, eds. *Proceedings of the Third Annual Symposium About Language and Society*. Austin, TX. 266–295.

Stevens, Kenneth N. 1998. *Acoustic Phonetics*. Cambridge, MA: MIT Press.

Stewart, Kathleen. 1996. *A Space on the Side of the Road: Cultural Poetics in an "Other" America*. Princeton, NJ: Princeton University Press.

Stockwell, Robert and Donka Minkova. 1997. "On drifts and shifts." *Studies in Anglica Posnaniensia* XXXI: 283–303.

——. 1999. *Explanations of Sound Change: Contradictions between Dialect Data and Theories of Chain Shifting*. Leeds Studies in English, New Series Vol. XXX: 82–103.

Strange, Winifred. 1999. "Perception of vowels: Dynamic constancy." In J.M. Pickett, ed. *Fundamentals of Speech Perception, Theory, and Technology*. Boston: Allyn & Bacon.

Strange, Winifred, T.R. Edman, and J.J. Jenkins. 1979. "Acoustic and phonological factors in vowel identification." *Journal of Experimental Psychology: Human Perception and Performance* 5(4): 643–656.

Sugrue, Thomas. 1996. *The Origins of the Urban Crisis: Race and Inequality in Post-War Detroit*. Princeton: Princeton University Press.

Thomas, Erik. 1991. "The origin of Canadian Raising in Ontario." *Canadian Journal of English Linguistics* 36. 147–170.

———. 1993. "Vowel changes in Columbus, Ohio." *Journal of English Linguistics* 22: 205–215.

———. 1995. *Phonetic Factors and Perceptual Reanalyses in Sound Change*. Ph.D. Dissertation. University of Texas, Austin, TX.

———. 2000. "Spectral differences in /ai/ offsets conditioned by voicing of the following consonant." *Journal of Phonetics* 28: 1–25.

———. 2001. *An Acoustic Analysis of Vowel Variation in New World English*. A Publication of the American Dialect Society 85. Durham: Duke University Press.

Thomason, Sarah. 2001. *Language Contact*. Edinburgh University Press.

Tillery, Jan and Guy Bailey. 2003. "Urbanization and Southern American English." In Stephen J. Nagle and Sara L. Sanders, eds. *English in the Southern United States*. Cambridge University Press. 159–172.

Trudgill, Peter. 1986. *Dialects in Contact*. Oxford: Blackwell.

Trudgill, Peter, Elizabeth Gordon, Gillian Lewis, and Margaret Maclagan. 2000. The role of drift in the formation of native-speaker southern hemisphere Englishes: Some New Zealand evidence. *Diachronica* 17(1): 111–138.

U.S. Bureau of the Census. 2000 U.S. Census Data. http://www.census.gov/

Watt, Dominic. 1998. *Variation and Change in the Vowel System of Tyneside English*. Ph.D. Dissertation. University of Newcastle upon Tyne.

———. 2000. "Phonetic parallels between the close-mid vowels of Tyneside English: are they internally or externally motivated?" *Language Variation and Change* 12(1): 69–101.

Widick, B. J. 1989. *Detroit: City of Race and Class Violence*. Detroit, MI: Wayne State University.

Williams, Cratis D. 1992. *Southern Mountain Speech*. Berea: Berea College Press.

Wolfram, Walt. 1969. *A Sociolinguistic Description of Detroit Negro Speech*. Washington, DC: Center for Applied Linguistics.

———. 1974. *Sociolinguistic Aspects of Assimilation: Puerto Rican English in New York City*. Washington, DC: Center for Applied Linguistics.

———. 2007. "Sociolinguistic Folklore in the Study of African American English." *Presentation at the Linguistic Society of America Annual Meeting*, Anaheim, CA.

Wolfram, Walt and Donna Christian. 1976. *Appalachian Speech*. Arlington: the Center for Applied Linguistics.

Wolfram, Walt and Erik Thomas. 2002. *The Development of African American English*. Oxford: Blackwell.

Wolfram, Walt and Natalie Schilling-Estes. 1998. *American English: Dialects and Variation*. Oxford: Blackwell.

Wolfram, Walt, Erik Thomas, and Elaine W. Green. 2000. "The regional context of earlier African-American speech: Evidence for reconstructing the development of AAVE." *Language and Society* 29: 315–355.

Woods, Anthony, Paul Fletcher, and Arthur Hughes. 1986. *Statistics in Language Studies*. Cambridge, England: Cambridge University Press.

Woolard, Kathryn A. 1998. "Introduction: Language ideology as a field of inquiry." In Bambi B. Schieffelin, Kathryn A. Woolard, and Paul V. Kroskrity, eds. *Language Ideologies: Practice and Theory*. New York: Oxford University Press. 3–47.

Woolard, Kathryn A. and Bambi Schieffelin. 1994. "Language Ideology." *Annual Review of Anthropology* 23: 55–82.

Index